Pre-Therapy

Pre-Therapy

Reaching contact-impaired clients

Garry Prouty

Dion Van Werde

Marlis Pörtner

PCCS BOOKS
Ross-on-Wye

First published in 2002

Previously published in German as
Prä-Therapie
(1998) by Klett-Cotta

PCCS BOOKS
Llangarron
Ross-on-Wye
Herefordshire
HR9 6PT
UK
Tel +44 (0)1989 77 07 07
email enquiries@pccsbks.globalnet.co.uk

Pre-Therapy: Reaching contact-impaired clients

British Library Cataloguing in Publication Data.
A catalogue record for this book is available from the British Library.

ISBN 1 898059 34 9

Cover design by Denis Postle
Printed by Bookcraft, Midsomer Norton, UK

Contents

The Authors

Dr. Garry Prouty, trained by Eugene Gendlin, is the founder of Pre-Therapy. He has lectured in Europe and north America in clinics, hospitals and training organisations for the past 17 years . He recently delivered the Frieda Fromm-Reichman Memorial Lecture at the Washington School of Psychiatry.

Garry Prouty has served as editorial consultant of the boards of *Psychotherapy, Theory, Research and Practice; The International Journal of Mental Imagery* and the newly-formed *Person-Centered and Experiential Psychotherapies* (the journal of the World Association for Person-Centered and Experiential Psychotherapy and Counselling). His other books include *Theoretical Evolutions in Person-Centered/Experiential Therapy: Applications to schizophrenic and retarded psychoses* (Praeger, 1994).

Dion Van Werde is a psychologist with a postgraduate specialisation in Client-Centered/Experiential Psychotherapy (K.U. Leuven). He is Pre-Therapy Staff Fellow of the Chicago Counseling and Psychotherapy Center, U.S.A. He is coordinator of the Pre-Therapy International Network, based at Psychiatrisch Ziekenhuis, St Camillus, Gent, Belgium, where he uses Pre-Therapy as a ward model in residential care for people diagnosed as psychotic.

Marlis Pörtner works as a psychologist and psychotherapist in private practice (among others with mentally impaired clients) and as a consultant for staff members of different social organisations. She has written and published numerous articles and several books *including Trust and Understanding: the Person-Centred Approach to everyday care for people with special needs.* (PCCS Books, 2000) She lives in Zürich, Switzerland.

Acknowledgements

This joint project of three authors from three different countries with three different languages has a long history — a history of encounter, involvement, mutual trust and friendship. We are grateful to each other for this, and our very cordial thanks go to all the others who contributed to the realisation of this project.

We thank Jill Prouty for her constant support.

We thank the Van Werde family for patience and support.

We thank the clinic Sint-Camillus, Gent, especially the board of 1987, Sr. Ludwig, Dr De Wilde and Mr Schelfaut, who made it possible for Dion Van Werde to study with Garry Prouty in Chicago and who — supported by Dr Dierick — invited Garry Prouty for a symposium at Sint-Camillus, on the occasion of the inauguration of the pre-therapeutically-oriented CONTACT ward.

We thank all those who participated in preparing this ward and consequently were working there: the psychiatrist Dr Claudine Mertens; the therapists Annemie Lippens and Etienne De Buck; the inspiring friend and colleague Chris Deleu; and the nurses Katrien De Meulemeester, Makstien De Rycke, Chris De Vos, Hilde Jacobs and Bea Segers. Sincere thanks also to those who joined the team later and committed themselves to the difficult task of taking care of psychotic patients in mutual understanding and close team work.

We thank the actual board of Sint-Camillus: Marc Vermeire, Sr Ludwig, Dr Claudine Mertens, Jan Steel and Bert Vanacker who, on the administrative level, increasingly safeguard the project and since 1996 host the yearly meeting of the Pre-Therapy International network.

We thank our colleagues who, in conversations and written reports, shared their experiences in working with Pre-Therapy: Helmuth Beutel, Ute Binder, Ton Coffeng, Aldo Dinacci, Michael Kief, Hermann Kolbe, Elke Lambers, Wim Lucieer, Hans Peters, Bart Santen.

We thank the psychiatric clinic Sint-Amandus in Beernem, near Bruges: particularly Dr Luc Roelens and the pre-therapy team Bea Coninckx, Leo Dumon and Chris Van Wyngene who, for an intensive week, allowed Marlis Pörtner to attend their work and in many different ways provided her with information and material. We thank the staff members Christine Adriaensens,

Ralf Bonte, Eric Buyck, Jeanine Carels, Hans Chielens, Johan De Brabander, Anne Degadt, Anita Hillewaere, Marie-Jeanne Hudders, Emmanuel Langerock, Marijke Magerman, Karen Neyt, André Roucourt, Koen Vanquaethem, Frank Verstraete and Philippe Veys for their hospitality and for giving information during this week. Above all, we thank the patients of Sint-Amandus who received the foreign visitor with courtsey and allowed her an insight into their life at the hospital. We thank Piet Labian for the beautiful poem he presented us with for this book.

We thank our German publishers Klett-Cotta, who first published this book, particularly Irmela Köstlin for competent and sensitive editing, and Roland Knappe for help and support in settling and formulating the complex contractual aspects of this joint project.

And last, but not least, our sincere thanks go to Maggie Taylor-Sanders and Pete Sanders for publishing this book at PCCS Books, thus making it available to English language readers.

Garry Prouty, Dion Van Werde and Marlis Pörtner

Foreword

Since the publication of this book in German and Dutch (Prouty, Van Werde and Pörtner, 1998; 2001), it has become clearer that Pre-Therapy is developing and making its own place in the therapeutic world.

The members of the Pre-Therapy Network International (founded in Amsterdam in 1995 and bringing together people who are interested in Pre-Therapy, in its critical evaluation, as well as in its spreading and development) will come together this year for the fifth time on a row in Gent, Belgium. These meetings are the beating heart of the Pre-Therapy movement and are the place where, with the participation of Garry and Jill Prouty, early experiences in new fields of application, education, research or theoretical issues can be shared and discussed. Topics in progress include a Danish Pre-Therapy project (L. Sommerbeck), the role of empathy (U. Binder) and Pre-Therapy and Dementia (I. Morton and P. Dodds). Not only does the number of people engaging themselves in Pre-Therapy increase, but also the number of applications, settings and target groups.

After Garry Prouty's first article (1976) and after his first book (1994), Pre-Therapy has grown in different directions. First, people other than those trained as 'Pre-Therapists' started to use contact-reflections. Publications emerged, written by nurses (Segers, 1999), labour therapists (Peeters, 1998) and even carers in home-settings (McWilliams and Prouty, 1998). Pre-Therapy influences are also reported in fields other than the care for psychotic people and the care for the mentally retarded. Ton Coffeng, for example, writes about trauma-therapy and working with the process of dissociation (1998, 2002). These are all expansions in the breadth of Pre-Therapy.

Secondly, Pre-Therapy has also been expanded further 'upwards' into working with people who function in the so called 'grey-zone'. This points at a level where psychotic and congruent functioning alternate or exist together (see Part 2 of this book). Thinking in terms of contact and contact-enhancing activities can even play a central role in thinking about psychological health in general and can bridge, or surmount, the supposed gap between, for example, patient and caregiver, and the sick and the healthy, (Pörtner, 2000; Van Werde, 2000).

We also see Pre-Therapy expanded 'downwards' to working with people who function on an even lower contact-level than the those Prouty worked with when designing his approach. We think about people who suffer from dementia, or even who are dying (Van Werde and Morton, 1999). When working with these latter target groups, of course, therapeutic ambition is necessarily limited; there, therapy is practised in maybe its purest form, namely as 'being with'.

At a more theoretical level, a number of topics have been addressed. Prouty (2000) wrote about the concept of 'pre-expressive self', about the differences between 'Rogerian' and 'experiential' therapy (Prouty 1999) and about humanistic research and therapy with schizophrenic people (Prouty, 2002). Deleu and Van Werde (1998) wrote about the relevance of a phenomenological attitude in working with psychotic people. Prouty made a summary of his work for the handbook of experiential psychotherapy by Greenberg, Watson and Lietaer, (1998). Peters (1999) wrote an overview of Pre-Therapy in the care for people who are mentally retarded for *The Journal of Humanistic Psychology*. All these recent publications show that Pre-Therapy continues to inspire an increasing number of people and is more alive than ever.

In his approach, Prouty makes space for the other and their universe. The sometimes pre-expressive and thus unintelligible utterances, by definition testify to a very personal and unique way of 'being in the world'. This needs and deserves to be approached with maximum care. The caregiver, or 'contact-facilitator', can do nothing more than — with existential empathy — offer himself to the other and thereby invite them to start the quest for 'relationship' and 'feeling' (Van Werde, 2002a). It is up to the client to decide whether someone is admitted to their world, whether they are willing to contact what is existentially present and if it can be shared. Ultimately, the contact-impaired client — whatever level he functions on (Van Werde 2002b) — is the only one who knows if, how and with whom he wants to travel this healing road.

Dion Van Werde
Autumn 2002

References

Coffeng, T. (1998) Pre-experiencing: a way to contact trauma and dissociation. *The Folio*, *17*, (1), 43–53.

Coffeng, T. (2002) Contact in the Therapy of trauma and Dissociation. In: Wyatt, G. and Sanders, P. (Eds.) *Rogers' Therapeutic Conditions: Evolution, Theory and Practice. Volume 4: Contact and Perception*. Ross-on-Wye: PCCS Books, pp.153–167.

Deleu, C. and Van Werde, D. (1998) The relevance of a phenomenological attitude when working with psychotic people. In: Thorne, B. and Lambers, E. (Eds), *Person- Centred Therapy: a European perspective*. London: Sage, pp. 206-15.

Mc Williams, K. and Prouty, G. (1998) Life enrichment of a profoundly retarded woman: an application of Pre-Therapy. *The Person-Centered Journal, 1,* 29–35.

Peeters, N. (1998) Ergotherapie bij psychosegevoelige mensen: een pre-therapeutische invalshoek (not published). Katholieke Hogeschool voor Gezondheidszorg, Oost-Vlaanderen, Gent .

Peters, H. (1999) Pre-Therapy: a client-centered experiential approach to mentally handicapped people'. *Journal of Humanistic Psychology,* 8–29.

Pörtner, M. (2000) *Trust and Understanding.* Ross-on-Wye: PCCS Books.

Prouty, G. (1976) Pre-Therapy — a method of treating pre-expressive psychotic and retarded patients. *Psychotherapy: Theory, Research and Practice, 13,* (3) 290–5.

Prouty, G. (1994) Theoretical *Evolutions in Person-Centered/Experiential Therapy. Applications to schizophrenic and retarded psychoses.* New York: Praeger.

Prouty, G. (1998) Pre-Therapy and pre-symbolic experiencing: evolutions in person-centered / experiential approaches to psychotic experience. In: Greenberg, L., Watson, J. and Lietaer, G. (Eds), *Handbook of Experiential Psychotherapy.* New York: Guilford Press, pp. 388–409.

Prouty, G. (2002) Client-centered/humanistic research and practice with schizophrenic persons . In: Cain, D. and Seeman, J. (Eds.), *Handbook of Research and Practice in Humanistic Psychotherapies.* Washington, DC: American Psychological Press.

Prouty, G. (2000) Pre-Therapy and the pre-expressive self. In: Merry, T. (Ed.), *The BAPCA Reader.* Ross-On-Wye: PCCS Books, pp. 68–76.

Prouty, G. (1999) Carl Rogers and experiential therapies: a dissonance?. *Person-Centred Practice, 6,* (2), 1–8.

Prouty, G., Van Werde, D. and Pörtner, M. (1998) *Prä-Therapie.* Stuttgart: Klett-Cotta.

Prouty, G., Van Werde, D. and Pörtner, M. (2001) *Pre-Therapie.* Maarssen: Elsevier gezondheidszorg.

Segers, B. (1999) Het herstel en de versteviging van het contact met de realiteit als focus van verpleegkundige zorg op een afdeling psychosenzorg (unpublished text). Vervolmakingscentrum voor verpleegkundigen en vroedvrouwen, Brussels.

Van Werde, D. (2000) 'Persoonsgerichte psychosenzorg: de tegenstelling "maatschappij" en "proces" overstegen?' *Tijdschrift Cliëntgerichte Psychotherapie, 28,* (4), 274–9.

Van Werde, D. (2002a) The falling man: Pre-Therapy applied to somatic hallucinating. *Person-Centred Practice, 10,* (2).

Van Werde, D. (2002b) Prouty's Pre-Therapy and contact-work with a broad range of persons' pre-expressive functioning. In: Wyatt, G. and Sanders, P. (Eds.) *Rogers' Therapeutic Conditions: Evolution, Theory and Practice. Volume 4: Contact and Perception.* Ross-on-Wye: PCCS Books, pp. 168–81

Van Werde, D. and Morton, I. (1999) The relevance of Prouty's Pre-Therapy to dementia care. In: Morton, I., *Person-Centred Approaches to Dementia Care.* Bicester, Oxon: Winslow Press, pp. 139–66.

Preface

The concept of Pre-Therapy, developed by the American psychologist Garry Prouty, is one of the most important evolutions in client-centred psychotherapy. Pre-Therapy opens access to people usually labelled 'not accessible by psychotherapy', such as long-term hospitalised chronic psychiatric patients, people with severe mental disabilities or with the so-called 'dual diagnosed': mentally disabled and mentally ill. Prouty's starting point is the 'psychological contact' between therapist and client that Carl Rogers has defined as one of the necessary conditions for a therapeutic process, and that with these clients is lacking. Prouty's method is based on the principle of 'reflections'; that is, the therapist is reflecting what he perceives. The first to use reflections in psychotherapy — on the cognitive level — was Otto Rank; he repeated what his clients were saying, in order to understand better their way of thinking. Carl Rogers expanded the use of reflections to the emotional level, in order to understand more accurately the feelings and experiences of his clients. Prouty has further developed this principle and uses reflections to help the clients to establish contact with reality, with themselves, with others.

Pre-Therapy proved not only to be a helpful instrument in psychotherapy, but also it can be used in different ways in the daily life of psychiatric clinics and homes for people with special needs. Therefore the concept is of interest not only for psychiatrists and psychologists, but also for anybody working in this field: carers, nurses, occupational therapists and others.

Prouty's Pre-Therapy has been tested and confirmed by various empirical research programmes. In Europe his approach has been picked up and elaborated, particularly in Belgium, Italy and the Netherlands, and, since 1992, also in Germany. This book, originally published in German in 1998, gives the first detailed description of Pre-Therapy, and its applications as well as its development in different countries.

In Part 1, Garry Prouty describes his personal history and the forming experiences that led him to create Pre-Therapy. He then explains the theoretical foundations and practice of Pre-Therapy, illustrated by using many examples. A separate chapter is dedicated to his theory of the pre-symbolic, throwing new light on the character of hallucinations. Prouty demonstrates how he integrates hallucinations and delusions into the therapeutic process and how, with this attitude and method, it is sometimes possible to reveal the original traumatic experiences which lie beneath.

In Part 2, Dion Van Werde, one of the pioneers of Pre-Therapy in Europe, describes the transformation of Prouty's individual approach into a ward setting. At the psychiatric 'Kliniek Sint-Camillus' in Gent (Belgium) where Van Werde works as a psychologist and psychotherapist, Pre-Therapy has been expanded to a 'milieu therapy'. One ward has been organised as a 'contact milieu' that shapes the different aspects of daily life. Van Werde takes into consideration organisational as well as therapeutic requirements. His approach is readily transferable to other organisations, as its principles can easily be adjusted both to different specific needs and to different general settings.

Van Werde's understanding of psychosis allows a therapeutic approach to patients, which is not set on the symptoms, but aims at 'anchoring' the person by facilitating and reinforcing their contact functions. The structures of the hospital offer a wide range of opportunities to do so: occupational therapy, movement therapy, leisure activities and also various aspects of daily life. Van Werde's achievement is truly pioneering work. Moreover it is up to now the only psychiatric ward worldwide that is entirely based on client-centred principles. The system that has been built up at Sint-Camillus proves that a person-centred, pre-therapeutic way of responding to patients is absolutely compatible with the structural requirements of an organisation, on condition that attention is paid to both aspects and that the constant challenge of finding an adequate balance between different — and sometimes diverging — interests is met.

The first chapter of Part 3 describes another long-term project at a psychiatric clinic, Sint-Amandus, in Beernem, Belgium. A week-long visit to the clinic in 1996 forms the basis for the detailed report of this programme for chronic psychiatric patients, and demonstrates how much more can be done for this usually neglected group of patients. Furthermore it highlights, in addition to the application of Pre-Therapy, how Prouty's ideas have changed the way staff in different areas of the clinic perform their daily work.

The second chapter of Part 3 gives a short overview of other developments in Europe. It summarises various approaches and applications of Pre-Therapy in several countries and different professional fields including psycho-therapeutic practice, psychiatric hospitals and organisations for people with special needs.

Prouty's concepts and the many ways to apply them offer a more humane alternative for taking care of psychiatric patients and people with special needs — not as a vague ideology, but in a quite concrete, practical and pragmatic way. We hope that many readers will be inspired by the variety of examples to think about how they could integrate elements of Pre-Therapy in their own specific professional field — not only for the benefit of the people they work for, but also for themselves as this can make their work more meaningful and more satisfying.

Marlis Pörtner

Part 1

Garry Prouty

The Foundations of Pre-Therapy

I wish to acknowledge another formative influence in the person of my wife Jill. This has been in the form of 'belief'. Many years ago, Jill believed in the work itself. I thought she was 'prejudiced'. The so-called prejudice turned out to be an affirmation of creative effort in the midst of a marital relationship. A rare gift!

Garry Prouty

Chapter 1

Formative Experiences

Pre-Therapy was born in a mix of painful feeling and experiences, developed through living with my retarded and mentally ill brother, 'Bobby'. There is no doubt that this complex gave birth to my creative efforts in psychotherapy. I use the Jungian term, *complex*, because more than the literal felt-sense is involved. The actual living experience is layered, having pain, empathy and a sense of defensive creativity.

There is a great deal of hurt attached to the memories of my brother; not having seen him for half a century. Today, the pain is too intense to seek contact with him. Recently, the state institution where he was a resident, unwittingly invited me to lecture on Pre-Therapy. I had to refuse, fearing the depth of the pain. That pain has the quality of 'being for him' and I know I carried empathic pain for his isolation. One memory is of Bobby sitting on our front porch with no-one to play with, rocking, holding his head and crying. Another tender memory concerns his little yellow footstool that was isolated in the corner of our house. He would sit there alone for hours. My regret, to this day, is that I did not play with him and give him more loving attention.

This loneliness, in retrospect, extended into his evening hours. In the evening, after I went to bed, I could hear him singing in his room. He would sing two songs over and over. The line I remember the most was, 'My heart cries for you, sighs for you'. At the time, as a youngster, I did not realise this was possibly his way of expressing the abandonment he was experiencing in the neighbourhood and family. Looking back is still grief-laden.

The impact of Bobby's disabilities tore the family apart. My parents would rage at each other, each blaming the other with guilty intent over family heredity. My mother deteriorated into alcoholism and religious fantasies. I can recall her standing by the radio trying to obtain healing 'vibrations' through the religious programme. Later she expanded this into frankly paranoid delusions concerning 'secret' messages coming from automobile lights on a nearby hill. My stepfather would take his rage and despair out on me, hating my intellectual interests (astrophysics, etc.). I literally have a dent in my skull from his beatings. The psychological results for me were a deep sense of worthlessness which impeded my growth and life for years to come.

Finally the family collapsed. First, because of conflict between my stepfather and myself, I was sent to live with my grandmother, who really did care about me. Bobby was sent to an institution for the rest of his life, and I never went back home. As I look back on my family, I feel a caring and realistic sense of pain.

During one of the experiences of physical cruelty in my family life, I developed a temporary bout of amnesia. It probably developed from head blows or a limited dissociation. The examining psychiatrist concluded I would probably recover; he also told my parents that I was a gifted child for whom every attempt at education should be made. No one understood the importance of this professional observation; no one had the background to understand it. My discussions of wanting to be an astrophysicist were considered unreal 'fancy' talk and were dismissed with contempt by my stepfather (who had to struggle with a retarded child). In addition, because we lived near the poverty level such aspirations were out of the question. The emphasis was on getting the usual manual job. To me this seemed like a doomed life of meaninglessness. It seemed impossible to become educated, given our economic situation and a strongly entrenched social inferiority which haunted me for years to come.

My spiritual core

In high school, while living with my grandmother I supported myself by working hard after school hours. My grandparents could not support themselves; they were at the poverty level. We hauled drinking water from a nearby mountain stream. We washed our clothes in rainwater. Snow came through the walls. I still remember waking up with snow on the bed. They were both ill and I worked long hours to finish high school. There was not sufficient money or time for household repairs; some of the windows were of wax paper. It is with mixed pride and shame I recall the school gave me a $5.00 reward for 'the student making the greatest gains against the greatest possible odds'. My grandfather finally succumbed to his cancer. I left my grandmother alone, left the rural mountain environment and took with me a precious psychological gift that no money could have purchased. A human empathy for poverty and my beloved grandmother's 'rock-ribbed' Protestant individualism were forever embedded in my soul. Today, these circumstances make me who I am and influence my sense of psychotherapy. My grandmother was a 'lay' preacher. I still picture the little church with the sounds of 'Rock of Ages' and 'Amazing Grace' moving over the green hills.

Something character-building came from this period, a certain spiritual attitude and a moral passion as a way of expressing God. I still remember how this influenced my choice of college course — the teaching of retarded children. I did not consciously realise I was bringing my earlier pain and later hardship together into a unity. I will never forget walking down the driveway, turning around and seeing my grandmother waving. I had $17 in my pocket, a bus ticket and excitement in my heart. The world was open. I never dreamed what was to follow, although I knew psychology was my path.

Teacher's college — self discovery

Life at the college was difficult and wonderful at the same time. It was coloured by a serious lack of money. The first year I shovelled garbage and cleaned tables at the college dormitories. The work was hard and dirty, yet somehow I was happy to be free to be moulding my own life. Working in the dorm cafeterias I received free meals and would take food home for storage in an outside window box. The second year I was promoted to pot washing. The college was socially wonderful to me. I met students from all religions and all ethnic origins. This certainly expanded my human horizons and dissolved the bigotry my parents had installed.

The most wonderful part of the college was being identified as a 'special student'. I took an introductory psychology course. The instructor was an older woman, a clinical psychologist, Dr Mazie Earl Wagner, a specialist in gifted children. She perceived my cultural impoverishment, yet sensed my potential. This all started because she had shown a film about gifted children at Hunter College. At seeing the children, the shock of self-recognition sent me out of the classroom crying. She was very compassionate with my pain. Realising my academic potential she asked me if I wanted to be tested; I agreed. After the test she said my reasoning capacities were beyond the scope of the test. I then told her that in high school I had invented a new geometric proof that my teacher had to send to specialists.

Interesting enough, further collaboration of Dr Wagner's assessment came from the science department of the college. For twenty-five years, the science instructor had been administering scientific reasoning tests and I received the highest score ever. At this point such 'discoveries' meant little to me. I wondered how they would help in getting me through my economic hardships. Also, these findings did not fit my self-image; I could not take them seriously given the circumstances of my day-to-day life. I never dreamed these abilities would become the dominant force in a creative theoretical life.

The next event at the college also came from Dr Wagner. She asked every instructor to enrich my studies and in a non-directive manner let me pursue my own interests. For science, I read the philosophy of science. For music, I listened to classical music for the first time in my life. For child development I made a first step in experimentation. The college actually allowed me to test and observe a retarded child in relation to a certain hypothesis I had. This was my first attempt to think seriously about retarded people. Of course I was naïve but the faculty encouraged my energy. I will always remember this small college and its dedicated faculty. They 'lit the fire' of my intellectual interest and passion; it transformed me. Dr Wagner was my surrogate 'good mother'.

My inner 'gifted child' needed a 'gifted mother'. She has since passed away and my regret is that she never got to know the results of her human investment. This experience formed my own teaching life of over 25 years. I could only pass on her gift to young students. I left that teachers' college after three years with a belief in my intellectual ability forever a part of myself. They had nurtured my soul far beyond formal education. Years later, I won a state level, college teaching award.

The university — intellectual passion

For the last year or so of undergraduate study, economic hardship was a big part of my life. My wife and baby slept on floors and often there was not enough money to take public transportation. I had transferred from teachers' college to a private university. It was there that 'naïvety' encountered 'intellectual greatness' and experienced the electricity of philosophical thought and tradition, through the person of Dr Marvin Farber, the American philosopher. In Germany, Dr Farber had been a direct student of Husserl. He had taken over the publication of the international phenomenological journal after Husserl's death during the war years. In addition, he had written many articles and books on phenomenology. When he lectured I felt the weight of history and tradition in his words. I had never seen or heard such intellectual depth before. I was too awed to ask for an appointment or to speak in class. I just absorbed the intellectual passion and charisma. When he described walking with Husserl in the forest, it was as though history was in every breath. Farber taught me the depths to which thinking could go; I was totally captivated. Forty-five years later, his specific teaching came to life in my use of his phenomenological naturalism and realism as the foundation of Pre-Therapy. I had kept the class notes for that length of time. And it took that long for me to understand the real meaning of his thought and decades to appreciate his disagreements with Husserl. He taught me freedom of thought, the nature of phenomenology, and the search for truth and intellectual humility. I never once talked directly to him. I felt too ignorant.

Upon entering graduate school I chose an interdisciplinary programme in social psychiatry. I encountered sociological thought in the form of symbolic interactionism. This, combined with actual hospital contact with psychiatric patients, started me on the long road to developing pre-symbolic theory. I was infatuated with perceiving man as a symbolic creature. I discovered the writings of Suzanne Langer and Ernst Cassirer. All of this eventually led to my later theoretical conception of hallucinatory symbols. These are my intellectual debts to this university.

However, one additional experience stands out. The graduate department of social psychiatry was small and all classes were run on a seminar basis, and it operated a system of non-directivity. Students were totally free to pursue their own interests. This taught me to guide my own intellectual life and to build my own process. Again, as with the teachers' college, I blossomed from the academic freedom. I learned to attack my own intellectual problems rather than serve the professor. I learned how to become an autonomous scholar and I learned intellectual joy with this freedom. Also, during this period, my fascination with schizophrenia started through hospital contacts and studying the impact of social class on this problem. At the end of several graduate semesters, I again, restlessly, transferred schools.

Eugene Gendlin — my mentor

The most decisive influence on my professional development was Eugene Gendlin, who influenced me on so many levels. It started with my searching the university catalogue for an evening class and finding a listing for existential psychology. Since I knew nothing about the subject I decided to take the class. Upon arrival there was no instructor present. We waited, and waited and waited. Finally after 45 minutes the elevator door opened; out stepped this man. I instantly recognised the genius in this person and was immediately fascinated by this philosopher–psychologist. I knew this would be a great professor. It was he who introduced me to Person-Centred/Experiential Psychotherapy, philosophical psychology and to humanism in therapy. I recall writing my first graduate paper on the different nature of experiencing between Gendlin and Rogers. I recall him saying, 'So that's how we are different'. Gendlin was available and encouraging. He would spend hours as I would fill the blackboard with attempts to frame my theoretical thinking about symbols and experience. I still remember one afternoon when he said I would make a contribution to psychology. Of course, I thought he was just a kindly teacher who liked me and I did not take his remarks seriously. The important thing was that I felt his creative regard and this helped me continue these embryonic efforts. He was my gifted, 'creative father'. He touched my creative therapeutic soul in a personal way.

The 'birth' of Pre-Therapy

Pre-Therapy was 'born' (1966) in a one-room workshop for retarded or mentally ill clients. This workshop was attached to the Kennedy School for Exceptional Children in Palos Park, Illinois; it made and packed candles and other light items. The clients had behaviour and employment-skills training. My role was to provide mental health counselling. The clients were mostly either retarded or were regarded as schizophrenic and the agency role was rehabilitative and therapeutic. The atmosphere in the agency was not at all sophisticated. For a time my office was inside a truck. My supervisor, Howard Weiss, had a client-centred background. He realised I was really working with clients in an intensive way and did a great deal to assist me. He suggested I ask Eugene

Gendlin to consult and Gendlin agreed.

At this point, three formative experiences came together, which led to the development of Pre-Therapy. First, I brought my person-centred/experiential training to the situation. Secondly, I brought my private experience with my brother to the therapy. And third, the low-functioning, regressed clients were available at the workshop. These elements combined without conscious thought and the Pre-Therapy mode emerged. It was natural and I could not sense the difference from classical Rogerian work. The fact I could work well with these clients caught Gendlin's attention and he began to question me about the work I was doing. I was convinced I was doing 'classical' person-centred/experiential therapy. I was totally inarticulate and could only say 'I respond'. To me, this was a self-evident statement and I could not see why it wasn't sufficient. I didn't realise that this 'responding' I was doing was different. I would argue with Gendlin that I was applying what I had been taught. He argued that he and Rogers did not seem to get these results. What was different? Gendlin became frustrated and for along time did not want to discuss anything further. At this point, I felt this pressure was unreasonable and decided to leave.

I changed jobs to teaching in a small college. Then the students began telling me my responses could not be found in either the Gendlin's or Rogers' reading assignments. Finally, relentless student questioning produced an articulation which I wrote down and Gendlin published. Seeing my 'way' published was totally beyond my sense of self. It was a wonderful shock.

Carl Rogers — my psychological hero

My first contact with Carl Rogers was through his writings. I saw him as a psychological revolutionary. I compared him with Martin Luther, in that Luther empowered the individual to define his moral reality and Rogers empowered the individual to define his psychological reality. He democratised the therapeutic relationship using client experiential knowledge instead of therapist theoretical knowledge. He helped people to have the courage and conviction to be themselves. The non-directive approach seemed to maximise the client's psychological freedom. These were the reasons why client-centred therapy seemed the only way for me. It was a question of values. I doubt if I will ever leave this 'home'. The core attitudes themselves did not fascinate me, they just seemed to be completely natural and obvious. How else would you relate to a client?

My first actual contact with Carl Rogers came in the early seventies. Gendlin suggested I phone him and let him know about my work. I remember how inappropriate I felt, yet I placed the phone call. I was stunned and tongue-tied. I remember asking if I were talking to *the* Carl Rogers. I said who I was and that Eugene Gendlin suggested I contact him. I explained I was doing work with people with learning disabilities or psychosis and asked if I could send a sample of my work. Rogers' reply was that he was not working with such clients and that I should send my work to someone else. He talked about how tired he was and how much work there was to do. I felt I was talking to Mount Olympus, but I realised I was receiving a kindly 'brush-off'. I was crushed, but some place in me got angry – I decided to persist. Later, I learned his refusal was consistent with lack of extensive experience with this population.

The next contact with Rogers came in 1986 and was quite eventful. The Chicago Counselling Centre invited him to participate at a symposium celebrating their anniversary. To everyone's delight, he accepted. The symposium consisted of Carl Rogers, Eugene Gendlin, Natalie Rogers, Nat Raskin and myself. Rogers spoke first, Gendlin followed and then my opportunity came next: I was terrified. It felt impossible to follow the two of them. History was there, in person, sitting at the same table. Practically, everything I knew about psychotherapy was there in the flesh. All I had learned was literally focused within ten feet. I had just finished a successful workshop in the Netherlands, so I took what little self-worth I could find and with some courage plunged forward. Some faculty members from my little college were there giving support. My wife and daughter were like emotional life rafts in a sea of strangers. My wife Jill still recounts that Rogers immediately started to take notes on what I was saying. What I presented was the work of one of my students (Mary Ann Kubiak) with a catatonic schizophrenic young man. It is now a classic case in Pre-Therapy. Publicly, Rogers said my work was important and I knew this was priceless recognition. However, it was the non-public contact that deepened that sense.

After my case presentation, a break was given for people to relax. I was drained from the earlier experience and was standing with my wife Jill and daughter Gwen. I was surprised to see Carl Rogers walking straight towards us. I introduced my wife and daughter and expected it to be a polite social contact; instead Rogers, in a very direct way, said, 'You killed the Bhudda'. I replied gently (my wife's recount): 'You have to love the Bhudda before you kill him'. He then walked a few steps, turned and said, 'Don't let the bastards get you down'. That was the communication; I have turned to it many times for strength.

Later we all had dinner together at a local restaurant. I remember Rogers saying he was tired and excusing himself. I remember his walking up a short flight of stairs to a small glassed-in porch and stepping outside into the darkness. I recall looking at him through the glass panes. The outside was dark. I saw him outlined against the stars. I 'knew' I would not see him again. My thought was what had been remarked at Lincoln's death – 'and now he belongs to the ages'. Carl Rogers died a few months later, leaving us the most humanistic psychology ever formulated.

In closing, perhaps there is a 'vital thread', an impulse, a picture, and a coherence. Maybe this therapeutic work is a living symbol of all the human efforts, influences and experiences I have tried to describe in this chapter. That is the sense of wholeness I have.

Chapter 2

Pre-Therapy and Existential Phenomenology

Towards a concrete phenomenology

Pre-Therapy is part of the phenomenological tradition in psychology and psychiatry (Husserl, 1977; Jaspers, 1963). In particular, Pre-Therapy is a 'pointing at the concrete' (Buber, 1964); when we say Pre-Therapy is focused on the concrete, we are referring to a particular way of 'seeing' lived experience. We are referring to a literal, perceived, immediate experience — this particular chair, this specific sound, this exact feeling. We are emphasising the approach because many therapists respond to general essences of symbolic meaning and not to what is there, what is existing. This is reminiscent of Rollo May's comments that existential psychology is characterised by a sense of reality and concreteness (May, 1983).

The 'As Itself': towards a philosophical understanding of the concrete

The 'As Itself' (Prouty, 1994) refers to the philosophical 'seeing' and an existential understanding of concrete lived experience. It is derived from a synthesis of the phenomenological writings of Sartre (1956), Farber (1959, 1967) and Scheler (1953).

The concreteness of experience 'as itself' is expressed by Sartre's description of experience as 'Absolutely Self-indicative'. This means that experience refers to itself or implies itself. In psychotherapy, the primary understanding is for the clients' literal experience, not interpreted experience. Many therapists do not respond to the actual lived experiencing of the client — they respond through their schemas about client experiencing.

Guideline 1: Try to respond to the direct experience of 'what is there', i.e. what is immediately perceived

The concreteness of experience 'as itself' is also expressed by Farber's description of the phenomenon as 'naturalistic'. This means describing the phenomenon 'as it appears' in consciousness, without excluding the naturalistic or realistic qualities. The affirmation of client reality is a helpful anchoring in the experiential fluidity of psychosis (Van Werde, 1994).

Guideline 2: Try to respond to the clients' naturalistic and realistic sense when it is present.

Finally, all of this co-ordinates with Scheler's belief that the phenomenon is *de-symbolised* This means that the phenomenon *as itself* is below the level of language. This gives us the alternative sensibility that sub-linguistic experience is manifested by the client, through bodily, facial and situational expression.

Guideline 3: A therapist needs to look as much as listen.

Towards a psychological understanding of concreteness

Concreteness is very important in understanding brain-damaged and psychotic experience. Gelb and Goldstein (Gurswitch, 1966) conducted a phenomenological experiment contrasting brain-damaged with normal clients. The results essentially described the damaged patients as perceiving shades in colour as *distinct separate* colours. The damaged clients were very literal and concrete. Thus their perceptual style was labelled 'concrete'. This essentially meant that the client's percepts were stimulus-bound. The normal subjects took *shades of the same colour as a single colour*. Their percepts were categorised, therefore labelled 'categorical'. This meant the client's percepts were abstracted essences.

The concrete style of perception was also noted by Arieti (1955); thus brain-damaged and psychotic clients perceive quite concretely. This is significantly basic to the Pre-Therapy method, which relies on extraordinarily concrete reflections. These reflections are concrete in that they are often oriented towards pre-verbal levels of expression and are quite literal and duplicative. This is often uncomfortable for normal clients to whom we 'categorically' listen. The Pre-Therapy method is adjusted to the concrete style of brain-damaged and psychotic clients.

The existential structures of consciousness

Traditionally, the Person-Centred/Experiential Approach to psychotherapy has concerned itself with experiential *process* (Rogers, 1961; Gendlin, 1964). Pre-Therapy is additionally concerned with the experiential *structures* of consciousness.

As a fundamental way of understanding the nature of human experience, Pre-Therapy returns to naturalistic, concrete consciousness as it is lived. Husserl described consciousness as *intentional*. This means consciousness is always about, towards, or with an experience. This is a basic function of consciousness. Next, Merleau-Ponty describes the phenomenal field of consciousness as the World, Self or Other. (Merleau-Ponty, 1962). Combining these philosophical notions with Farber's naturalism, one can understand ordinary, everyday, natural consciousness as about, towards or with the world, self or other. I live with, and consciously experience, the World in all its immanent power. I live with, and experience, the Self with all of its psychological value. I live with, and consciously experience, the Other with all its significance. This describes the 'existential' structures of consciousness. They are the 'polarities of involvement' for our life. They are the 'revelatory absolutes' of our existence.

In addition, the existential structures of consciousness function as the *contact* structures of consciousness. They are the 'contact mechanism' between consciousness and experience. The contact between consciousness and experience is *existential contact*. The lack of contact between consciousness and experience is *existential autism*. This autism is observable in schizophrenia (Arieti, 1955; Minkowski, 1970). Pre-Therapy, in existential–phenomenological terms, is the movement from *existential autism* to *existential contact* with world, self or other.

Existential empathy

Existential empathy is for the human condition, psychotic or not. It is a 'bearing witness' to human suffering with humility and acceptance. It is an openness to agony and destruction beyond healing. It is where the last response is to 'be with'. This is an important attitude in working with 'psychologically terminal' clients. It is the defeated therapist coming to terms with realising all he has to offer is his own simple *humanity*. I observed this in a Glasgow workshop where a minister was grieving at not being able to sustain therapy with clients suffering from Alzheimer's disease. This was due to their increasing organic deterioration. The man collapsed, sobbing in spiritual pain. After experiencing his grief and sense of failure, he realised an acceptance of psychological death. His ministering became a peaceful 'being with' the nothingness. This is a difficult lesson for therapists.

Chapter 3

The Theory of Pre-Therapy

Introduction

Pre-Therapy is an evolution in person-centred thinking and practice. Rogers' approach to therapy is usually expressed through the core conditions (Rogers, 1957). These conditions or attitudes are described as unconditional positive regard, empathy and congruence. Unconditional positive regard is defined as having a warm, accepting and caring attitude towards the client, no matter what. Empathy is an accurately-expressed understanding of the client's experience. Congruence is described as the emotional genuineness of the therapist with the client. The presence and expression of these attitudes, in combination with a non-directive reflection of the client's feelings and meanings, are considered the essence of Client-Centred Therapy. This blending of attitude and technique is conceived as facilitating the self-formative or actualising tendency of the client (Rogers, 1978).

Rogers defines psychological contact as the first condition of a therapeutic relationship (Rogers, 1959). This 'first condition' is regularly overlooked, with research emphasis being on the 'core conditions' (Watson, 1984). Further, Prouty (1990) describes Rogers' use of psychological contact as based on assumptions and lacking in definition as well as technique. In the light of these issues, Pre-Therapy is the development of a theory and practice of psychological contact. Pre-Therapy is used for clients who cannot utilise relationships because they are *contact impaired*.

Psychological contact
Psychological contact is described on three levels:
   Contact Reflections, the work the therapist does.
   Contact Functions, the client's process.
   Improvement in contact is measured by *Contact Behaviours.*

Contact Reflections
Contact Reflections are the techniques of empathic contact; they are applied when there is not sufficient contact to implement psychotherapy. They provide the contact between therapist and client when the client is incapable of Reality, Affective or Communicative Contact. Contact Reflections are very literal,

concrete and duplicative. They are sensitive to the concrete expressive particularity of the client's regressed behaviour. This emphasis is required because of the often pre-verbal or sub-verbal nature of chronic schizophrenic, geriatric, psychotic or handicapped populations. There are five contact Reflections:

- Situational Reflections (SR)
- Facial Reflections (FR)
- Body Reflections (BR)
- Word-for-Word Reflections (WWR)
- Reiterative Reflections (RR)

Situational Reflections (SR). The therapist looks at the client's current situation, environment or milieu and reflects the client's related behaviour. For example: the patient is staring at a spot on the floor. The therapist might reflect, 'You are looking at the large spot on the floor.' Simpler examples might be 'Paul is holding a cup', or 'Paul is touching the table'. These types of reflection facilitate Reality Contact. In a training workshop, a social worker was role-playing with a client and, of course, eventually herself. For an entire hour she did not respond to Contact Reflections. Finally, I reflected her looking out of the window at the rain. She replied, 'The rain is like my inside tears'. This, of course, opened up more feelings.

Facial Reflections (FR). The therapist looks at the client's face and observes pre-expressive affect. An example would be, 'Paul smiles', or 'Paul looks angry'. These types of reflection facilitate affective contact. These are often necessary with regressed clients because excessive tranquillisation, psychosocial isolation, or institutionalisation lead to an atrophy or defensive numbing of affective expression.

Body Reflections (BR). Often psychotic or retarded clients exhibit various bizarre body postures, gestures and movements. These may take the form of echopraxia, catatonic posturing, etc. The therapist may reflect them verbally or bodily. A verbal example is, 'Paul's body is stiff', or 'Paul is rocking'. A non-verbal example can be drawn from the case of a depressed handicapped person. The therapist describes the client as entering the room and driving an imaginary car. The client would turn the steering wheel and bend over as the car turned around corners. The therapist would reflect these body motions by duplicating and sharing the body movements of turning the corner. These reflections help the client live in his body and overcome the bodily alienation many regressed people experience.

Word-for-Word Reflections (WWR). Many psychotic clients often function at a sub-verbal level, expressing word fragments, incomplete sentences, or isolated words. They also exhibit symptoms such as echolalia, word salads or neologisms. The therapist listens carefully and reflects the word, even if he does not understand its meaning. The person is 'received' as a communicator and very often expands their message. An example is as follows: '(Incoherence) . . . run, (incoherence) . . . tree, (incoherence) . . . paper'. The therapist would reflect the three understood words. Occasionally, the therapist may reflect a non-verbal sound. These reflections help develop communicative contact.

Reiterative Reflections (RR). Reiterative reflections embody the principal of *re-contact.* If a previous reflection worked, repeat the reflection. There are short term and longer-term reiterations. An example of immediate re-contact is illustrated from the therapy of a schizophrenic man. The therapist reflects, 'You smiled' (silence of several minutes). The therapist reiterates, 'You are still smiling' (re-contact). The client then congruently says, 'Happy'. A longer-term reiteration occurred with the treatment of a schizo-affective, handicapped woman. The therapist reiterates, 'Last week you said, "baby", now you are rocking the doll as though you are holding a baby'. The client moved into expressing more about babies. This further processed into a real abortion experience.

These five techniques consist of providing the client with a 'web of contact' at different levels, thus allowing the client opportunities of expression and relatedness. All of these assist the client to move from a pre-expressive state to an expressive state, allowing the client access to psychotherapy.

Contact Functions

The Contact Functions represent an expansion of Perls' concept of 'contact as an ego function' (Perls, 1969). These are labelled Reality, Affective and Communicative Contact. They are conceived as awareness functions and form the theoretical goals of Pre-Therapy. The purpose of Pre-Therapy is the restoration or development of Reality, Affective or Communicative Contact.

Reality Contact is described as the awareness of the 'world'. Specifically, this means the awareness of people, places, things and events. Our 'world' is 'peopled' both in the subjective and objective sense. Subjectively, we have internalised significant others in varying degrees. Objectively, we contact people in offices, airlines, streets, etc. People are a part of our reality structure. We are spatial creatures also. For us, everything is in a place. 'My book is there', 'You are here', etc. This is also part of our reality structure. In addition, 'things' are definitely part of our reality. There are books, trees, computers, houses, coffee pots, belt buckles, the sun and stars, false teeth, grass, etc. Humans are in a constant relationship with things. Events are temporal. 'I will go to Washington in April, yesterday I went to the shops'; 'You came yesterday, I will go tomorrow'; 'You did it then; you are doing it now'. Time is also a part of our reality structure.

Affective Contact is described as the awareness of moods, feelings and emotions. Moods are subtle and diffuse, for example, 'I am in a depressed mood today'.

It is a colouring of affective experience; I may not know the origins of my mood, yet it is present. Feelings are specific, more clearly circumscribed, are more present, and clearly have an 'object' — 'I am depressed today because I have so little time for entertainment.' Emotions are more intense and usually linked to an event: 'If you hit my grandmother I will have an intense emotion, possibly blinding rage or pain.' Affective contact is always with the 'Self'.

Communicative Contact is the symbolisation of reality (world) and affects (self) to others through words or sentences. It is more than the transmission of information. It is the meaningful expression of our perceived world and self to others. Communicative Contact primarily refers to social language. It is a part of our 'Being in the World'. We live in language, we think in language, we even die in language (tombstones). One merely has to live in a foreign culture to grasp the psychological significance of language. Communicative Contact is always with the 'Other'.

Vignette

The following illustrates the development of the Contact Functions through the use of Contact Reflections (Prouty, 1994). The client was a woman with a chronic schizophrenic diagnosis who had been hospitalised for over thirty years. She was one of many clients on the ward who were milling around aimlessly. This particular description was between her and a young student who was becoming oriented to psychotic patients in a custodial institution. It illustrates the *pre-relationship* aspect of Pre-Therapy and the emergence of Reality, Affective and Communicative Contact as psychological function.

Dorothy is an old woman who is one of the most regressed women on the ward. She was mumbling something (as she usually did). This time I could hear certain words in her confusion. I reflected only the words I could clearly understand. After about ten minutes, I could hear a complete sentence.

D		**Come with me.**
T	(WWR)	**Come with me.**
		[Dorothy led me to the corner of the day room. We stood there silently for what seemed to be a very long time. Since I couldn't communicate with her I watched her body movements and closely reflected these.]
D		*[Dorothy put her hand on the wall.]*
		Cold.
T	(WW, BR)	*[I put my hand on the wall and repeated the word.]*
		Cold.
		[She had been holding my hand all along, but when I reflected her, she would tighten her grip. Dorothy began to mumble word fragments. I was careful to reflect only the words I could understand. What she was saying began to make sense.]

D		**I don't know what this is any more.**

D   **I don't know what this is any more.**
           [Touching the wall (Reality Contact).]
           The walls and chairs don't mean anything anymore.
           [(Existential autism).]
T (WW, BR) *[Touching the wall]*
           You don't know what this is anymore. The chairs and walls don't mean anything to you anymore.
D   *[Dorothy began to cry (Affective Contact). After a while she began to talk again. This time she spoke clearly (communicative Contact).]*
           I don't like it here. I'm so tired . . . so tired.
T (WWR)   *[I gently touched her arm. This time it was I who tightened my grip on her hand I reflected.]*
           You're so tired, so tired.
D   *[Dorothy smiled and told me to sit in a chair directly in front of her and began to braid my hair.]*

This case also ilustrates another aspect of Pre-Therapy — the movement from a pre-expressive to an expressive state.

Contact behaviours
Contact behaviours are the emergent behavioural changes that result from the facilitation of the Contact Functions through the use of Contact Reflections. The resulting behaviour dimensions are operationalised as Reality, Affective and Communicative Contact. Reality Contact is defined as the verbalisation of people, places, things and events. Affective Contact is described as the use of feeling words (sad, happy) or the behavioural expression of affect through the body (kicking a chair) or through the face (looking frightened). Communicative Contact is the use of words and/or sentences. These expressive dimensions are recorded, transcribed and scored. The formal hypothesis predicts increases in Reality, Affective and Communicative Contact. In general, and using slightly different configurations of measurement, pilot studies have found evidence supporting Pre-Therapy. These include significant increases in *theorised directions* (Hinterkopf, Prouty and Brunswick, 1979; Prouty, 1990), reliability (DeVre, 1992), *construct validity* (Prouty, 1994), *theorised increases* and reliability (Dinacci, 1994; 1995).

Pre-Therapy theoretically fulfils Rogers' conception of psychological contact as the first condition of a therapeutic relationship. It provides definitions, techniques and behavioural measurements. It is a systematic expansion of Client-Centred Therapy to contact-impaired clients.

The Pre-Expressive Self

The Pre-Expressive Self is a heuristic notion based primarily on the empirical and clinical study of Pre-Therapy. It is a construct that organises this information into an interpretation that is fundamental to understanding the process of Pre-Therapy and the expressive structure of regressive phenomena. Prouty (1997), describes the Pre-Expressive Self as a *meta-psychological* concept that refers to the propensity, for yet to be integrated experience, to form expression. It can be interpreted as an aspect of the self-formative tendency (Rogers, 1978).

Observations

The first level of observation concerning pre-expressivity involves a semiotic understanding of schizophrenic communication. Often these clients express themselves verbally in a manner that *appears* meaningless. Their verbalisation often seems to lack a context or a realistic referent. This style of communication appears 'without reality'. For example, a psychotic client suddenly expressed 'priests are devils'. This has no contextual reference and therefore appears to have no reality. Through Word-for-Word Reflections, this thought fragment unfolded into a real experience concerning a homosexual occurrence with a priest. It was germane to the development of the psychosis. The thought fragment contained 'the potential realistic meaning'. The therapeutic movement was from a pre-expressive state without realistic context to an *expressive* state with realistic context.

Next, actual case studies illustrate another meaning of pre-expressive. These cases illustrate communication that uses isolated single words, sentence fragments, thought fragments, neologisms, word salad, echolalia and lack of context or referents. These case studies document the client's struggle from a pre-expressive, sub-verbal state to utilising social communication. Additionally, pilot studies (Hinterkopf, Prouty and Brunswick, 1979; DeVre, 1992; Prouty, 1990, 1994; Dinacci, 1994, 1995), reveal a quantitative continuum from a pre-expressive to an expressive state.

Lastly, clinical vignettes (Prouty, 1994) describe withdrawn and isolated clients who immediately move from a non-contactful, pre-expressive state into full contact and expressivity. Although this shift is sudden, it still reveals the same pattern of movement from a pre-expressive to an expressive state. These anecdotes illustrate the presence of a self that experiences contact and suddenly emerges. Apparently, what is involved is a Pre-Expressive Self that is eclipsed by regression, autism, retardation, psychosis, dementia and communicative disorders, etc.

All of these observations imply that the therapist's attitudes include empathy for a client's efforts at moving from a pre-expressive to an expressive state as part of their self-formative nature. This is particularly true if the self-formative tendency is actualised in a therapeutic relationship.

In conclusion, the psychoanalytic concept of regression simply does not illuminate the possibility of pre-expressive potentials. The concept of psychotic regression is developmentally descriptive and is not a therapeutic concept. Regression and pre-expressive are polar opposite assumptions about low-functioning clients. They differ significantly about the potentiating possibilities for therapy with poorly integrated clients.

Chapter 4

The Practice of Pre-Therapy

Catatonia

The practice of Pre-Therapy is well documented in several 'classical' case studies. Among them is a case concerning the treatment of a catatonic young man who was restored to contact in a singular twelve-hour process (Prouty and Kubiak, 1988a). The client was a twenty-two-year-old male with several hospitalisations. He was one of thirteen children who lived on a large prairie farm in Canada. One sibling, although not 'officially' diagnosed, clearly presented psychotic symptoms. Further, the mother had been hospitalised several times as a schizophrenic. The client was brought to the USA for an evaluation by this author. I decided to attempt the case because contact reflections elicited some minimal communication. In addition, the psychotic hospitalisations were episodic, the client having not evolved to a total chronicity. Further, the client was young, thus falling into a better prognostic category. He was released from the Canadian psychiatric hospital and sent home without medications. This gave the unusual opportunity of treatment from a purely psychological frame. This case was 'presented' to Carl Rogers during a symposium held at the University of Chicago in 1986. This actual vignette and the total therapy were done by Mary Ann Kubiak.

Vignette

According to the psychiatric history, the client had been described as 'mute, autistic, catatonic, making no eye contact, exhibiting trance-like behaviour, stuporous, confused, not establishing rapport, delusional, paranoid and finally, experiencing severe thought blocking'.

He had been diagnosed variously as manic-depressive, hysterical reaction, hebephrenic schizophrenic, paranoid schizophrenic, catatonic schizophrenic, profound schizophrenic, schizophrenic-affective type. He had received six electroshock treatments, as well as numerous chemical interventions, including Stelazine, Diazapem, Impramine, Chloropromazine, Anafril, Phenothiazine, Haldol and Trifluioperazme.

The client was returned home for several months while residential care was developed, along with legal details. My associate (Kubiak) arrived in Canada and found that the client had been returned home without medications. He had deteriorated into a severe catatonic state, having withdrawn into the lower portion of his home. He did not eat meals with the family, only creeping out at night to use the family refrigerator. He had lost considerable weight and his feet were blue from being cramped and stiff from his lack of movement.

This vignette describes segments of a 12-hour process that illustrates the application of contact reflections, the successful resolution of a catatonic state, and the development of communicative contact (without medications). The patient was sitting on a long couch, very rigid, with arms outstretched, even with his shoulders. His eyes were straight ahead, his face was mask-like and his hands and feet were blue-grey. The therapist sat on the opposite side of the couch, giving no eye contact to the patient. Reflections were given five to ten minutes apart.

Segment I (approximately 2 p.m.)

Therapist (SR)		**I can hear the children playing . . .**
T	(SR)	**It is very cool down here . . .**
T	(SR)	**I can here people talking in the kitchen . . .**
T	(SR)	**I'm sitting with you in the lower level of your house.**
T	(SR)	**I can hear the dog barking.**
T	(BR)	**Your body is very rigid.**
T	(BR)	**You are sitting very still.**
T	(BR)	**You are looking straight ahead.**
T	(BR)	**You are sitting on the couch in a very upright position.**
T	(BR)	**Your body isn't moving. Your arms are in the air.**
Client		*[No response, no movement.]*

The therapist brought a chair and sat directly in front of the patient and mirrored his body exactly as she saw it.

Segment II (approximately 3.30 p.m.)

T	(BR)	**Your body is very rigid. You are sitting on the couch and not moving.**
		[Approximately 15-20 minutes later.]
T		**I can no longer hold my arms outstretched. My arms are tired.**
C		*[No response, no movement.]*
T	(BR)	**Your body is very stiff.**
T	(BR)	**Your arms are outstretched.**
T	(BR)	**Your body isn't moving.**
C		*[Put his hands on his head, as if to hold his head, and spoke in a barely audible whisper.]*

		My head hurts me when my father speaks.
T	(WWR)	**My head hurts me when my father speaks.**
T	(BR)	*[Therapist put her hands as if to hold her head.]*
T	(RR, WWR)	**My head hurts when my father speaks.**
C		*[Continued to hold head for two to three hours.]*

Segment III (approximately 8 p.m.)

T	(SR)	**It's evening. We are in the lower level of your home.**
T	(BR)	**Your body is very rigid.**
T	(BR)	**Your hands are holding your head.**
T	(RR, WWR)	**My head hurts when my father speaks.**
C		*[Immediately he dropped his hands to his knees and looked directly into the therapist's eyes.]*
T	(BR)	**You've taken your hands from your head and placed them on your knees.**
		You are looking right into my eyes.
C		*[Sat motionless for hours.]*
T	(RR, BR)	**You dropped your hands from your head to your knees.**
T	(SR)	**You are looking straight into my eyes.**
C		*[Immediately he speaks in a barely audible whisper.]*
		Priests are devils.
T	(WWR)	**Priests are devils.**
T	(BR)	**Your hands are on your knees.**
T	(SR)	**You are looking right into me eyes.**
T	(BR)	**Your body is very rigid.**
C		*[He speaks in a barely audible whisper.]*
		My brothers can't forgive me.
T	(WWR)	**My brothers can't forgive me.**
C		*[Sat motionless for approximately an hour.]*

Segment IV (approximately 1.45 a.m.)

T	(SR)	**It is very quiet.**
T	(SR)	**You are in the lower level of the house.**
T	(SR)	**It is evening.**
T	(BR)	**Your body is very rigid.**
C		*[Immediately, in slow motion, puts his hand over his heart and talks.]*
		My heart is wooden.
T	(BR, WWR)	*[In slow motion, put her hand over her heart and talks.]*
		My heart is wooden.
C		*[Feet start to move.]*
T	(BR)	**Your feet are starting to move.**
C		*[More eye movement.]*

The therapist took the patient's hand and lifted him to stand. They began to walk. The patient walked with the therapist around the farm and in a normal conversational mode spoke about the different animals. He brought the therapist to newborn puppies and lifted one to hold. The client had good eye contact. The client continued to maintain communicative contact over the next four days and was able to transfer planes and negotiate with Customs officers on the way to the USA. He was able to sign himself into the residential treatment facility where he underwent classical Person-Centred/Experiential Psychotherapy.

This vignette illustrates the function of Pre-Therapy, which is to restore the client's psychological contact, enabling treatment. Very clearly, this client's reality and communicative contact were improved sufficiently to enter psychotherapy.

Crisis intervention

Another 'classic' case involves a crisis episode with a client who was dual-diagnosed as hebephrenic-schizophrenic and mentally retarded (Prouty and Kubiak, 1988a). She lived in a residential treatment facility. The paraprofessional therapist (now professional) was taking a group of clients on a community visit. The psychotic crisis occurred while they were driving in the van with a second staff person.

Vignette

The client was one of seven on a community visit from the residential facility. She was sitting in the rear seat of the van. Looking in the rear-view mirror, I saw the client crouching down with one arm in the air, outstretched over her head. The client's face was filled with terror. Her voice was escalating in screams.

I parked the van off the road and asked the other staff member to take the rest of the clients out of the van. I sat directly next to the client in her seat. Her eyes were closed and she was wincing in fear.

Client		*[In rising voice.]*
		It's pulling me in.
T	(WWR)	**It's pulling me in.**
C		*[Continuing to slip farther down into the seat, with left arm outstretched. Eyes still closed.]*
T	(BR)	**Your body is slipping down into the seat. Your arm is in the air.**
T	(SR)	**We are in the van. You are sitting next to me.**
C		*[Screaming.]*
T	(FR)	**You are screaming, Carol.**

C		**It's pulling me in.**
T	(WWR)	**It's pulling you in.**
T	(SR)	**Carol, we are in the van. You are sitting next to me.**
T	(FR)	**Something is frightening you. You are screaming.**
C		*[Patient screaming.]*
		It's sucking me in.
T	(WWR)	**It's sucking you in.**
T	(SR, BR)	**We are in the van, Carol. You are sitting next to me. Your arm is in the air.**
C		*[Beginning to sob very hard. Arms dropped to lap.]*
		It was the vacuum cleaner.
T	(WWR)	**It was the vacuum cleaner.**
C		*[Direct eye contact.]*
		She did it with the vacuum cleaner.
		[Continued in a normal tone of voice.]
		I thought it was gone. She used to turn on the vacuum cleaner when I was bad and put the hose right on my arm. I thought it sucked it in.
		[Less sobbing. It should be noted that daily, this patient would kiss her arm up to her elbow and stroke it continually.]
T	(WWR)	**Your arm is still here. It didn't get sucked into the vacuum cleaner.**
C		*[Smiled and was held by therapist.]*

Later that afternoon, a psychotherapy session was held and the client began to delve into her feelings about punishment received as a child. The kissing and stroking of the arm ceased. This vignette illustrates how the client was helped to deal with the acute episode in a psychologically beneficial manner without medications. The client was able to experience how her symptoms of arm kissing and stroking related to a negative childhood emotional trauma of her mother threatening her with a vacuum cleaner. In addition, the client was able to use this newly integrated material as a basis for further therapy concerning her mother.

Profound retardation and depression

The client was a twenty-one-year-old male and a resident of a state institution. He was profoundly retarded with a Stanford Binet mental age of two years and four months. His IQ was 13. Because of severe symptoms, he was not eligible for vocational or educational training. Also, he was not eligible for cottage activities or field trips. His symptoms included mood swings, crying, psychomotor retardation, and obsessive stereotypic grass pulling.

Medical records showed that the client had minor cerebral palsy and a history of slow motor development, sitting up at age fourteen months and walking at twenty-two months. The parents were of low-income, low socio-economic status. The alcoholic father physically and emotionally abused the boy during early childhood. This resulted in the mother divorcing the father and being forced to place the boy in a state institution. The mother maintained good contact with the boy, becoming part of parent advocacy at the facility.

The case is important because the psychological treatment was completed without medications, thus allowing a clearer evaluation. Previous medications had been Prolixin, Thorazine, Mellaril, and Vistaril. All medications were stopped at the beginning of Pre-Therapy. As a result of treatment, symptoms, decreased and more realistic communication developed. This was confirmed by objective data and the client became eligible for programmes within the institution.

Vignette

Early treatment autistic phase — therapist report

Treatment sessions were 30 minutes, twice weekly. 'During our first sessions, X would come loping into the room, sit down in a chair, and start driving an imaginary car. He would hold his hands and arms as on a steering wheel. (I later introduced a toy steering wheel.) He made clicking noises (turning signals) and engine noises ('vroom') over and over during the session. He would pretend to turn the wheel and bend sideways until he was touching the floor with his hand, shoulder or arm. Sometimes he would make great crashing noises and say 'beep-beep'. He drove continually and constantly during sessions for approximately the first year. There was very little eye contact during this time.

Typical session

Therapist		Hi, X.
T	(SR)	You're looking at the steering wheel.
T	(SR)	X is sitting in the chair, holding the steering wheel.
T	(SR)	We're both sitting in brown chairs.
Client		Vroom.
T	(WWR)	Vroom.
C		Click, click.
T	(WWR)	Click, click.
T	(SR)	X is turning the steering wheel.
T	(BR)	Arms crossing.
		[Crosses arms.]
T	(BR)	Body bending in chair.
		[Bends.]
C		Vroom, vroom.
T	(WWR)	Vroom, vroom.
T	(SR)	Our heads are touching the floor.

T	(BR)	We are bending over.
T	(FR)	You are looking.
T	(SR)	You are looking at the steering wheel.
C		Eee, kruss, sss.
T	(WWR)	Eee, kruss, sss.
T	(SR)	You're making crashing noises.
C		Click, click.
T	(WWR)	Click, click.
T	(SR)	You're making signal noises.
T	(SR)	We're sitting in a big room.
T	(SR)	The sun is shining.
T	(BR)	We're facing each other.
T	(BR)	Your arms are turning.
T	(BR)	*[Hands on steering wheel.]*
T	(BR)	You do, I do.
T	(FR)	X is smiling.
T	(SR)	X has been driving for a long time.
T	(RR)	Last time we were together, we were in a small room.
T	(FR)	You look sad.
T	(SR)	You are making crashing sounds.
T	(BR)	You do, I do.
C		Vroom, vroom.
T	(WWR)	Vroom, vroom.
C		Beep, beep.
T	(WWR)	Beep, beep.
T	(RR)	Last time we were together, you had a red shirt on.
T	(SR)	Today you have a yellow shirt.
C		Vroom, vroom.
T	(WWR)	Vroom, vroom.
C		Vroom, vroom.
T	(WWR)	Vroom, vroom.

Mid-treatment relatedness phase — therapist report

Gradually, the client became aware that I was reflecting his verbalisations and body movements. As we started to make contact he would drive, giving me eye contact and smiling as I did contact reflections. He would contort his body so his head was on the floor; however, he was seated in the chair, making driving sounds and actions. He would look to be sure I was giving contact reflections. We spent a lot of time driving, turning corners so that our upper bodies were almost on the floor, while our backsides remained in the chairs. As the driving behaviours slowly decreased, he would play with cars and other toys. I brought a large unbreakable mirror to the sessions. He would make faces into it and simultaneously watch his image while watching my reflections of his facial expressions. We played with a toy whose different shapes fit into holes of the same shape. At first, he played only with the basic toy and he had trouble fitting the shapes successfully. From there he moved to fitting the shapes in easily and then became uninterested in the toy altogether. He liked to draw and continued to enjoy playing with cars. His crying behaviour was diminishing in the cottage. During all this time I used only Pre-Therapy contact reflections.

T		Hi, X.
C		Hi, Mimi.
T	(SR)	You looked at Mindy when you said hi.
T	(SR)	You sit in chair.
T	(SR)	You're looking for the steering wheel.
T	(FR)	You look all around.
T	(SR)	You picked up steering wheel.
T	(FR)	You're smiling.
C		Vroom, vroom.
T	(WWR)	Vroom, vroom.
T	(FR)	You watch Mindy.
T	(SR)	The big mirror is on the table.
T	(FR)	You stick out your tongue.
T	(RR)	You do, I do.
T	(FR)	You smile when Mindy sticks out her tongue.
T	(SR)	We are both looking in the mirror.
T	(BR)	X and Mindy are sitting next to each other.
T	(SR)	X and Mindy look into the mirror.
T	(FR)	X smiles.
T	(FR)	You smile, I smile.
T	(FR)	Your lips are turned down.
T	(SR)	You are looking at X in the mirror.
T	(FR)	X is frowning.
C		Here.
T	(WWR)	Here.
T	(FR)	Now your lip is turned up.
T	(FR)	You do, I do.
T	(FR)	X is smiling.
T	(SR)	You pick up the steering wheel.
C		Vroom, vroom.
T	(WWR)	Vroom, vroom.
C		Vroom, vroom.
T	(WWR)	Vroom, vroom.
T	(SR)	You look in the mirror.
T	(RR)	You used to drive all the time.
T	(SR)	Now you drive sometimes.
T	(SR)	You pick up the red and blue toy.
T	(SR)	You're turning the toy around in your hands.
T	(SR)	You hand me the toy.

C		Open.
T	(FR)	You look.
T	(FR)	You look at Mindy.
T	(SR)	You want to take the shapes out of the toy.
T	(FR)	You watch.
T	(RR)	Last time we were sitting in the chairs.
T	(RR)	Last time it was raining.
T	(SR)	Today the sun is shining.
T	(RR)	Before, X said, 'Open.'
C		Here.
T	(WWR)	Here.
T	(SR)	You want the triangle in the hole.
T	(FR)	X smiles.
T	(BR)	You do, I do.

Ending treatment expressive phase — therapist report
In the ending phase of therapy, X's driving behaviour was extinct as was his crying behaviour. He no longer tore up the grass and he took part in a pre-vocational programme. He went home from our sessions without the aid of staff. During our sessions he was more verbal and more assertive, expressing higher self-esteem. He would walk around the room and ask basic questions. He would express emotions appropriately and knew when he was happy or sad. He was able to attend field trips. He would even talk about other people, showing much improved reality contact and social communication.

T		Hi, X.
C		Fine.
T		How are you today?
C		Fine.
T	(WWR)	Fine.
T	(SR)	You're taking off your coat.
T	(SR)	You are looking at Mindy.
C		Hang up?
T	(WWR)	Hang up?
T	(SR)	You want to know what to do with your coat. You can put it over there.
T	(SR)	You put your coat on the chair.
T	(SR)	You're walking across the room.
T	(BR)	You sit down.
T	(SR)	You put your arms on the table.
T	(BR)	You do, I do.
T	(SR)	You reach in the bag.
T	(SR)	X takes out the green car.
C		Vroom, vroom.
T	(WWR)	Vroom, vroom.

T	(SR)	X pushes the car off the table.
T	(SR)	It flies across the room.
T	(FR)	X laughs.
T	(BR)	X stands up.
T	(SR)	X pushes chair back.
T	(SR)	X picks up car.
T	(SR)	You're walking to the candy machine.
T	(SR)	You're rattling the handle.
C		Candy.
T	(WWR)	Candy.
C		Candy.
		[Louder]
T	(WWR)	Candy.
T	(SR)	X wants candy.
T	(SR)	No candy now, X.
T	(SR)	You're looking at Mindy.
T	(BR)	You're walking.
T	(SR)	You're looking at the stuff on the counter.
C		Plates.
T	(WWR)	Plates.
C		Napkins.
T	(WWR)	Napkins.
C		Party?
T	(WWR)	Party.
T	(SR)	You want to know if there is going to be a party?
T	(SR)	Christmas is coming.
C		Santa.
T	(WWR)	Santa.
T	(SR)	Santa comes at Christmas.
T		What are you doing for Christmas?
C		Going home in car.
T	(WWR)	Going home in car.
C		See Mom.
T	(WWR)	See Mom.
T	(RR)	You'll see Mom when you go home for Christmas.
T	(RR)	Before you laughed when you pushed the car off the table.
T	(FR)	You smiled when Mindy says that.
T		Is someone coming to take you back to your house?
C		No.
T		Good-bye, X.
C		Good-bye, Mimi.

A four-year follow-up review showed a stabilised and improved adjustment. The client was still without psychiatric medications. Institutional records indicate the client's accessibility to programmatic services. He participates in vocational, educational, and social activities. However, records also indicate instances of crying and verbal aggression.

An interview with his mother revealed her impressions: 'He's improved a lot . . . I really think it helped him a lot . . . We can bring him home now for longer periods of time without as much stress . . . It worked great.' Most interestingly, she reported, 'It helped him see himself.' His mother also wished the treatment could have continued longer if circumstances could have permitted.

Practice points

The preceding case vignettes are examples of direct contact reflections with clients. However, over a period of time, additional, more subtle practice points have evolved.

Empathic looking and seeing

Since *concreteness* is an essential aspect of Pre-Therapy (see p. 11), looking and seeing are important. Looking is the active visual seeking of experience; seeing is the visual reception of experience. Looking is intrinsic to the Situational Reflection. For example, an autistic client with severe echolalia is gazing at a calendar. The therapist, actively looking, reflects this. The client responds with congruent expressions about the various figures in the calendar, thus breaking the echolalic pattern. Looking and seeing are also important for Facial Reflections. The therapist needs to look directly at the facial expressivity of the client. They need to see the pre-expressive affect not yet formed into words, but present in the face. An example of this is taken from Roy (Prouty, 1994), who uses Pre-Therapy with multiple personality clients. She looked at the client's face and reflected 'angry'. Later, the client reported this helped her make contact with implicit anger of which she was not aware. Finally, looking is crucial in the use of body reflections. The therapist needs to attend to bodily expressions and reflect these see the case of catatonia p. 21.)

The non-responsive client

Contact Reflections frequently have impact for the client, whether there is a verbal response or not. Often this is *expressed* in subtle responses such as withdrawing the body, facial expressions, or even inaudible sounds or eye blinks. These are very tiny responses and often not noticed by the therapist. Often students will say 'nothing is happening'. This is not true. Often they have failed to see the *tiny responses*. These tiny expressive steps may provide an additional opportunity for contact. For example, a client may be sitting close to a therapist. The therapist may reflect, 'You are sitting close'. This may make this particular client uncomfortable or frighten him. It could be important to capture this by reflecting, 'You moved a little' or 'You look a little anxious'. These contacts may open more expression from the client. In Chapter 3, p. 16, I described a situation where I reflected the client looking out of the window at the rain. This led to the client saying the rain was like her depressed tears.

Personal nouns and pronouns

Pietrzak observed the autistic aspects of the psychotic/retarded and chronic schizophrenic clients (Prouty, 1994). She reported the use of first names in contact reflections, e.g. 'John waved his arms'. This observation emerged intuitively and probably helped form the basic identity at a safe psychological distance. More direct pronouns such as 'you' may be a little too intimate for clients for whom relationships may be threatening. This is in direct contrast to the Gestalt principle (Passons, 1975), which stresses the direct owning of self-experience. A similar observation is noticed in treating hallucinations. This therapist often uses the pronoun 'it' in regard to visual hallucinations. This provides semantic distance and a little more psychological safety in approaching the material.

Spatiality and temporality

Other concerns involve spatiality and temporality (Binswanger, 1958). Often, experiences of time and space are distorted. One client reports being terrified of time stopping. Another reports terror of rooms shrinking. The phenomenology of time slows during depressive episodes and accelerates during manic phases. Spatial phenomenology is frequently altered in hallucinatory states because hallucinations occupy literal space (Havens, 1962). Consequently, hallucinatory space becomes a sensitive dimension of contact. The tempo of contact is also important. Rapidly given contact reflections may be overwhelming. Conversely, too few reflections, given too slowly, may cause a lack of contact. It is important to understand the therapist is entering the phenomenological 'lived world' of the client and that one needs to be sensitive to the experiential structures of that 'being in the world'.

Self-formative effort

Often in working with regressed clients who are pre-expressive, the therapist does not know the client's frame of reference. They do not have enough phenomenological experience from which to form an empathic picture of the client's frame of reference. The empathy, then, needs to be inclusive of the client's *efforts* to cohere language and experience. The self is trying to form itself, albeit at a primitive level.

Chapter 5

Pre-Symbolic Theory

The problem

Gendlin (1964) provides descriptive definitions for his theory of experiencing. Accordingly, experiencing is a *concrete, bodily felt process,* which is the primary element in therapeutic change. The term 'concrete' is defined as experience to which a person can directly refer. Experiencing also has the quality of being 'bodily felt'. It is sensed and experienced in the organism. Lastly, the term 'process' refers to a bodily felt Experience A — shifting or moving to a new bodily felt Experience B. These components form the meaning of *experiential process.*

Gendlin describes hallucinations as *structure-bound* experiencing. The concept of structure-bound contains several levels of meaning. First, hallucinations are perceived 'as such' and 'not his' by the client. This describes the client's tendency to perceive hallucinations as literal reality. Second, the particular hallucinatory experience is *isolated.* The hallucination is not included in the felt functioning of the organism. Third, the implicit felt functioning is *rigid,* not in experiential process. This isolation and rigidity result in a loss of self-sense. Finally, structure-bound experiencing is static, repetitious, and unmodifiable.

Clearly, hallucinations are conceptualised by Gendlin as structure-bound — or, as one may say, a *non-process structure.* The theoretical and therapeutic problem is how to transform the hallucination from a non-process structure into a process structure.

The primacy of the symbol

The shift from a non-process structure involves a philosophical shift from lived experience to the symbolisation of lived experience — a shift from phenomenology to semiotics. This philosophical primacy of the symbol is asserted by Cassirer (1955) who describes humankind as 'Animal Symbolicum'. This means humans are conceived as symbolic animals. The vast superstructure of culture, science, philosophy, religion, etc., are thought of as symbolic structures.

This philosophical impulse is given further articulation through the work of Suzanne Langer (1961). She describes the human brain as a 'transformer'. The brain transforms 'the current of experience into symbols'. These metaphors permit us to think of human beings as motivated to symbolise experience.

Semiotics

The multiple ways in which humanity symbolises its experience is called the science of semiotics. Reichenbach (Szasz, 1961) describes levels of symbolising experience in terms of abstractness and concreteness. The most abstract form of symbolising experience is called the 'meta-symbol'. Meta-symbols are exemplified by scientific and philosophical terms. An example is $E = mc^2$. This term does not directly refer to a lived experience. It is an abstract expression of a physical process beyond experience. Another example of a meta-symbol is Christianity; no one can experience all of Christianity. The symbols of logic are another example of the meta-symbol. They refer to other symbols and not to lived experience. Meta-symbols are extremely abstract.

The next level of symbolising experience is called *object language*. It is ordinary cultural speech. This level of abstraction is described as a word referring to a concrete object. For example, the word 'book' refers to the concrete object and the word 'cow' refers to the literal animal.

Continuing along the abstractness–concreteness continuum is the *indexical sign*. The indexical sign is a concrete experience that refers to a concrete experience. For example, in nature the concrete experience 'cloud' refers to the concrete experience 'rain'. The perspiration of a person refers to the hot sun.

An even more concrete symbolisation of experience is the *iconic sign*. An iconic sign is a literal duplicate of the referent e.g. a photograph or a phonograph record. These are exact copies of their referent; they are symbolic duplicates.

A more primitive form of concreteness is the pre-symbol (Prouty, 1986). It 'cannot be clarified by something else' and 'it is inseparable from what it symbolises' (Jaspers, 1971).

The meaning of pre-symbol

The term 'pre-symbol' refers to the structure of the hallucinatory image, as separate from its processing. Psychotherapy with schizophrenic patients reveals that hallucinatory images contain both symbolic and phenomenological properties. This creates a definitional polarity.

Sartre (1956), as stated earlier, described the phenomena as an experience that is 'absolutely self-indicative'; an experience refers to itself or means itself. Whitehead (1927) described a symbol as 'an experience that indicates another experience'. Symbols are experiences that refer to another experience, or that mean another experience.

In essence, the phenomenon is 'about itself' and the symbol is 'about something else'. The co-existence of these polarities requires a synthesis to describe fully the structural reality of the hallucination. This is the basis for the term 'pre-symbol'.

Theoretical concepts

The hallucination as pre-symbol exhibits three attributes or properties: expressive, phenomenological and symbolic.

Expressive
As an expressive structure, the hallucination is described as 'self-intentional'. As already mentioned, Langer (1961) views the human brain as a 'transformer', something that transforms the *current of experience* into symbols. This motivational metaphor allows us to think of the hallucination as an expressive transformation of real-life experience into image form. One client described the essence of this self-intentionality, saying, 'These images are my unconscious trying to express itself.' Another client described it as 'the past trying to come back'. Still another conveyed this volitional quality by saying, 'The images start in my unconscious and move toward my consciousness to become real.'

Phenomenological
As a phenomenological-experiential structure, the hallucination is described as 'self-indicating'. It is experienced as real and, as such, it implies itself. Experience A implies Experience A. The hallucination *means itself as itself*

Symbolic
As a symbolic structure, the hallucination is described as 'self-referential'. As a symbol, it is an experience that implies another experience. Experience A implies Experience B. The hallucinatory image (Experience A) contains its referent (Experience B) within itself. The hallucinatory image *means itself within itself.*

As psychological fact, do hallucinations concretely possess the properties of being self-intentional, self-indicating and self-referential?

Pre-symbolics: discovery-oriented psychotherapy

Mahrer (1992) describes the difference between hypothesis-oriented psychotherapy research and discovery-oriented psychotherapy. The former is concerned with research design and statistical assessment, the latter with clinical discovery. This discovery approach is illustrated by Boss (1963, 1980), who found hallucinations to be significant in the psychotherapy of schizophrenia.

The major discovery of Pre-Symbolic psychotherapy is that schizophrenic hallucinatory experiencing leads to the integration of reality-based 'not-conscious' experiences.

Four examples of working with pre-symbolic experiencing

Example 1
The following vignette shows how Pre-Therapy is deeply rooted in the Rogerian approach, and illustrates the self-intentional, self-indicating and self-referential properties of the hallucinations.

Vignette (Prouty, 1991)

The client, a male age 19, was diagnosed as moderately retarded (Stanford-Binet IQ of 65). He was from upper-lower-class origin of Polish ethnicity. There was no mental illness in his family, and the client had not been diagnosed or treated for mental illness; that is, he was not receiving any medications for psychosis. He was a day-client in a vocational rehabilitation workshop for the mentally retarded. He was referred to me for therapy because of his severe withdrawal and non-communication. The client also behaved as though he was very frightened. He was shaking and trembling at his workstation and during his bus ride to the facility. At home, he rarely talked with his parents and he never socialised with neighbourhood peers.

During the early phases of therapy, the client expressed almost nothing and made very little contact with me. He was very frightened during the sessions and could barely tolerate being in the room with me. Gradually, with the aid of contact reflections, the client accepted a minimal relationship and expressed himself in a minimal way. Eventually, it became clear the client was terrorised by hallucinations that were constantly present to him.

The following description provides an account of Pre-Symbolic Experiencing. It provides an outline of hallucinatory movement and its subsequent resolution about its origins.

Phase I: 'The purple demon'

Client   It's very evil, this thing. What it wants to do is to rip me apart, you know. It's very evil . . . and it's very evil, this thing. It wants to rip me apart, but it's very evil, this thing. That's why I don't want anything to do with it. I'm tempted by it, you know. It's so small, but it has so much strength and it wants to rip me apart, you know. It wants to drive me into the past. It wants . . . it wants to make the past come back and I don't want the past to come back like it did a long time ago. It's over with, you know. It's

	not coming back anymore. The past doesn't come back; it's over with already.
Therapist	It's evil and strong. It wants the past to come back.
C	This evil thing is a picture. It's a purple picture that hangs there. It just hangs and I can see it. I can see it . . . the picture, you know. It's purple, it's very dark. It's very dark. So I can see it and I don't like it. I don't like it at all. It's very dark.
Therapist	It's a dark purple picture and you don't like it.
C	And . . . it's very tempted and I don't want to be tempted by it. It's very small. It's very evil, you know . . . that's all . . . It just hangs there. It don't do nothing. It's very evil. It's tempted. I'm tempted by it and it's very evil, you know. It's just like a picture. A purple picture. It just stays there. It just stays there, you know, the picture . . . It don't do nothing, it's evil, you know. I don't like it at all. It's not good and this thing, whatever it is. It's in the past and it's very strong, the past . . . And it's over with and it's not coming back any more. The past doesn't come back, and this is like now. It ain't the past, you know. It's over with and I don't want to be tempted by it any more. Yeh, yeh . . . it's very evil, very evil and very strong and has a lot of strength to it.
T	It's evil and it's in the past. It's strong and it hangs there. You don't want to be tempted by it.
C	This thing, you know . . . this thing has a very lot of strength to it. It's evil, you know. This thing has a very lot of strength to it. It's evil. It's not good and that's why it's very evil, this thing.
	[Pained laughter.]
	It's over with. It's the past, and it's not coming back any more. It's over with a long time ago, you know. It's not going to come back any more. I used to talk about the trees and the flowers, grass, and it's all over with. It's not coming back any more. It's something else, the picture. The purple picture just hangs there. It's evil. No?
T	The purple picture just hangs there. It's evil and you don't like it.
C	The past, it came from the past and the past is over with. It's not coming back any more, you know.
T	It comes from the past.
C	It's a picture. It's just a picture. A big purple picture. It just hangs there. I don't think it will rip me apart. I think it's very strong, but it ain't going to rip me apart, I don't think it will rip me apart at all, no.

T   It's a big purple picture. It won't rip you apart.

C   This thing is getting big and large. It's very big and large. It wants to get me. I won't let it. It's evil. It's like a demon, a bad demon. It wants to chop me all up. I won't let it chop me all up because it's bad. Very bad
[Loud sobs.]
Just a temptation, like any other temptation. A temptation is a temptation. You shouldn't be tempted by it and you know I want to pull away from it. I don't want to go by it.

T   It's big and large and evil. It wants to chop you. It's very tempting.

C   It's very bad and it's very destructive. It ain't good at all by it. It's like a bad demon, like a . . . like a demon or evil or something. Like a demon devil and I don't care for it too much. You know, at all. I . . . I don't like it too much, no. I don't like it at all, this thing. It's very bad and very evil, you know. It ain't no good. It's very bad. It's with the past and it's not going to come back any more. It's over with, you know, and talking about the trees and the flowers and grass and that's over. I mean, it's not coming back, but this is right now, I mean.

T   It's bad and destructive, like a demon devil. It's evil and with the past.

C   It's not coming back, but this is right here now. I can feel it, you know. It's like air. It's up above me. It's very up above and I can feel . . . almost touch it, you know. It's so close, very close. It's like a demon, you know, demon devil or something. 'Ho, ho, hoing' and all like that, you know . . . very bad, very bad. It forces me, pressing, very pressing on me . . . It's very pressing, it forces, a lot of force to it and it wants to grab me, you know. It wants to grab me. The feeling wants to grab me. The feeling wants to grab me.

T   It's very close and it wants to grab you.

C   The feeling . . . the feeling . . . ah, it's in the picture. The feeling is in the picture. Yes, it's there and I can see it. I don't like it. It's over with, you know. It's like the past and it's not coming back any more. It's over. It's just the trees and flowers and grass and that's over and it's not coming back.

Phase 1 describes a purple demonic image that just 'hangs there'. The client experiences it as evil and powerful. The image is considered destructive and wants to rip the client apart. This phase contains the property of being self-intentional. The client expresses:

'It wants to drive me into the past. It wants to make the past come back and I don't want the past to come back like it did a long time ago . . . It's over with, you know . . . It's not coming back any more . . . The past doesn't come back, it's over already.. It's in the past and it's very strong, the past and it's over with and it's not coming back any more . . . The past doesn't come back and this is like now... It ain't the past, you know . . . It's over with and I don't want to be tempted by it . . . It's in the past and it's not coming back any more.'

As illustrated by this example, 'self-intentional' means the expressive transformation of real-life experiences into images.

Phase II: 'Orange Square Hate'

C	It's orange, the colour's in a square. It's an orange colour that's square and it hates me. And it don't even like me. It hates me.
T	It's orange and it's square and it hates you.
C	It hates me a lot, you know, and it scares me. I get scared because of that. I get scared because it hates me.
T	It's orange and it's square and you get scared a lot.
C	And because it's orange, that scares me and I get scared of the bad hating.
T	The orange and bad hating scare you a lot. That hate scares you.
C	I get scared because of that. I get scared a lot. I get scared of the orange thing. It's orange.
T	You get scared of the orange thing.
C	Big orange, square thing. It's square and it's orange and I hate it. It don't like me because it hates me. It hates me and I get scared and I get excited over it too. I get very excited.
T	You get very excited.
C	It's exciting, I'm excited over it too. I do, I do. I get excited over it a lot. What? I get scared a lot about it. It makes noises. It makes noises.
T	It's orange and it makes noises.
C	It makes noises . . . It hates me. It also gets me excited. It gets me excited. It does, it gets me very excited a lot. I get, I get, I get very excited over it. I do, I do. I do. There's so much hate and it scares me and it makes me uncomfortable. It does. And it's real . . . It's real, it is.
T	It's real.
C	It is, it's very real.
T	It's very real . . . You point to it. It's over on your side. You

	see it.
C	I see it. Over there, over there.
T	It's over there.
C	It makes sounds, too.

Phase II has an image that is orange, square, and has hate in it. The client is very frightened of it. Phase II contains self-indicating properties because it is experienced as real, as a phenomenon. It implies itself. The client's process is as follows: 'and it's real, it is . . . It is, it's very real . . . I see it . . . Over there . . . Over there . . . It makes sounds, too.'

Phase III: 'Mean lady'

C	Yeah, well. Yeah, I would. I would. She's . . . I don't know. There we go. What? What?
	[Auditory hallucination.]
T	Okay, let's talk about what you see.
C	Well, she ain't real, you know, and she ain't real, you know. What?
	[Auditory hallucination.]
	Ha, ha, ha.
	[Sobs.]
	She has orange hair and yellow eyes.
T	She has orange hair and yellow eyes.
C	She's very pretty. She's very pretty. She loves getting mean when I am bad. She could get . . . she's mean, you know.
T	She's pretty and mean.
C	She is. She is. No, really she is. Really she is . . . with yellow eyes and orange hair. Boy! That scares me. That scares me a lot. That scares me a lot . . . Yeah, both the meanness and the . . . What?
	[Auditory hallucination]
	Yeah. Aah, I can see it and I don't even want to see it. It's over with and it's not coming back any more. I can even see it.
T	You can see it.
C	Yeah, that scares me. Yeah, it does. I think about it. I think it scares me.
T	When you think about it, that scares you.
C	I get scared. I don't want to think about it. I got it. I got it.
T	You don't want to think about it, but you got it.
C	I got it. It's orange, you know. That's helping, she's helping.
T	She's helping.

C	She scares me though, she scares me. But as long as I'm good, but as long as I'm good, I am . . . she's a friend.
T	As long as you're good, she's a friend.
C	But she's scary.
T	She's scary.
C	Scary. Yellow eyes, orange hair she has, she does. Reminds me of a dragon, you know. Her eyes are like that.
T	Her eyes are like a dragon.
C	Almost, you know, like a dragon . . . Her eyes are like a dragon . . . She's strong . . . She's strong, I'm weak. And I'm good, but she's also mean. She can be mean, too, see? And I'm good, if I'm good and I am, I really am, but she's all . . . she's very mean. She can be mean . . . and it scares me.
T	She's mean and that scares you.
C	She looks over me. She watches over me, but she has eyes like a dragon . . . Right. That's like a dragon and then she scares me and I get scared.

At this point, the client appeared upset and wanted the tape recorder turned off. Over the next two sessions, the image processed into a nun who had beaten the retarded client because he did not understand his school lessons.

Phase III contains an image of a woman that the client describes as pretty, mean and scary. She has orange hair and yellow eyes. This deeply frightens the client. The significant theoretical observation of this phase is its processing to its experience of origin. The client recaptures a real memory of being beaten by a nun who punished him for not completing his school lessons. This phase illustrates the self-referential property of hallucinations; that is, it symbolises an experience within itself. It refers to an 'originating' event (the nun).

Example 2

I have also described the hallucination as a process structure (Prouty, 1977). These vignettes of several clients describe stages of Pre-Symbolic Experiencing in the form of a process typology. These stages of experiencing parallel and further validate the 'process conception of psychotherapy' (Rogers, 1961). The hallucination moves from 'a fixity and remoteness' of self-experience to 'a clear, alive, immediate and integrated' self-experience. The stages of hallucinatory experiencing are described as the self-indicating stage; the self-emotive stage; the self-processing stage; and the self-integrating stage.

Self-indicating stage

This stage displays a hallucinatory image that signifies itself. It implies and refers to its own existence; it draws attention. The hallucinatory image has signifiers that stand forth and appear energised, that possess some intensity of colour or shape or movement.

'I see the upper left corner of a square. The lines are yellow, like a bright light shining through the navy blue. The navy blue is so dark it is almost black. The lines sway around, left to right, forward and backward. There is no pattern in the movement.'

During the self-indicating stage, the therapeutic technique needs to be directed towards the image itself. Such a focus is desirable in order to make the primary process more perceptually stable and, hence, more accessible to client and therapist. Such technique is labelled *image reflecting*.

Image reflecting refers to the reflection of literal, self-indicating properties of the image or symbol itself. In the previous examples, the following imagistic properties would be reflected:
• 'Like a bright light shining.'
• 'It's so dark.'
• 'The lines sway around, left to right, forward and backward.'

During the self-indicating stage, the hallucination is mostly symbolic, and little manifest affect is present. To initiate the development of feeling it is necessary to maximise the interactive effect of reflecting and experiencing. It may be necessary to repeat image reflections over and over before feelings begin to emerge from the hallucination.

Self-emotive stage
At this point, affect has developed in or around the hallucinatory image as part of its own self-signification or as a result of reiteration.

'It's like a painting. Like a picture on the wall, or a painting with feelings — it's like a painting on the wall, only with feelings in it' (from Prouty, 1966).

Reflecting in the self-emotive stage is towards both the image and the feeling in order to maintain 'process unity' (Gendlin, 1964). If either image or feeling is over-reflected or under-reflected, the total process will split, and the client will experience either a proliferation of images with little feeling, or a density of affect with no emotional process. In the example cited, the therapist would reflect, 'It's like a painting' (image) and, 'There are feelings in it' (feeling).

In another example, the client's hallucination is an 'orange square, with anger in it.' The therapist would reflect 'orange square' (image), and, 'There is anger in it' (feeling). If both the image and feeling are reflected and reiterated, both will evolve and process unity will be maintained.

Self-processing stage
During this stage, both image and affect process, and there is a shift from symbolic (image) to non-symbolic experiencing (feelings).

'I'm crying huddled in a chair. Garry comes by and I hold on to him. I am afraid. The object has changed from the corner of a square to a head on a stick. It's a man's head. There is a cape on a stick. It is suspended in air. It moves close and then goes back. God, I can't stand it, he . . . no, it couldn't be true, please, anything but this . . . he . . . no . . . no . . . no . . . he didn't do it to me, Lord, not my dad. I loved him. He . . . he . . . no, I won't believe it . . . he tried to kill me.'

In the example cited, symbolic and emotional processes are illustrated, as well as the sequential and proportional shift from symbolic content to feeling content:

Symbolic (image) process and content:
• The object has changed from the corner of a square to a head on a stick.
• It's a man's head.
• There is a cape.
• It moves back and forth.

Feeling process and content:
• Can't stand it.
• Can't be true.
• Please . . . he didn't.
• Not my dad.
• I loved him.
• I won't believe it.
• He tried to kill me.

In the self-processing stage, reflections begin to change proportionally from the reiterative-symbolic modality to a more classic client-centred concern with feeling. This change is caused by an evolution from a 'fixity and remoteness of experience to a clear, alive, immediate, integrated experience' (Rogers, 1961). In essence, there is a shift from symbolic experiencing (image) to non-symbolic experiencing (feeling), and the reflective modality changes along with it.

Self-integrating stage
In this stage, affect shifts from the hallucinatory image to the person's own sense of self, and is integrated, owned, and experienced as self.
'It was at this point that the image was no longer merely an external story. But very rapidly I realised that the child was myself. It was impossible to hold back the flow of feeling accompanying the image. It was like being one's self and staring at one's self in the same instant. I felt the fright the child in the image was experiencing.'

At this point, reflections are generally much more focused on the feeling process. Since the patient has assimilated and integrated the ego-alien hallucinations, the therapist can shift to traditional client-centred/experiential responses.

Example 3
The following example (Prouty and Pietrzak, 1988) describes the application of the Pre-Therapy technique (contact reflections) to the hallucinatory experience.

Vignette

'Michael', a divorced and recently re-married man in his sixties, was referred as an outpatient. His original diagnosis was phobic-neurosis; however, the referring psychiatrist described the client as experiencing an acute depressive episode and was concerned over possible hospitalisation for a developing schizophrenic psychosis. The client was not receiving medication. Presenting symptoms were intense, vivid images that the client periodically experienced as real. Corresponding physical problems were sweating, increased blood pressure, tremors, and other physical manifestations of anxiety. Frequently, these symptoms rendered the client non-functional. These symptoms occurred after the client married his 'common law' wife of several years. The client reported no such symptomatology during 30 years of previous marriage or during other intimate relationships.

Michael experienced images of being drowned, and of people without faces being hurt. He reported feelings of being in a dangerous situation that he could not explain.

C		It's like I'm drowning.
T		You're drowning.
C		Yeah.
T	(RR)	It's like you're drowning.
C		Can't figure it . . . where I am.
T	(FR)	Where are you? Your face is twisted.
C		Where . . . it's horrible.
T	(BR)	It's horrible, you're moving all over.
C		It's like I'm drowning. Yes, it's me.
T	(WWR)	It's you.
C		It's me drowning. It's not big; it's a bathtub or something.
T	(WWR)	It's you . . . bathtub or something.
C		I can't breathe.
		[C, hands to throat.]
T	(BR)	It's choking you.
		[T, hands to throat.]
C		It's all over . . . faces, it's all over.
T	(WWR)	It's all over.
C		Black clear people.
T	(WWR)	Black clear people.
C		Cold. It's getting me.
T	(WWR)	Cold. It's getting me.

	(RR)	It's all over.
C		It's me in a bathtub. Faces. I'm in a bathtub.
T	(WWR)	You're in a bathtub.
		[Long pause.]
C		I'm in a bathtub. I'm drowning. Faces, people, are they getting hurt?
T	(WWR)	It's you in a bathtub.
C		It's me . . . what's happening? It's getting me. I'm drowning. The faces are ugly.
T	(BR)	You turn away. You're drowning . . . ugly.
C		It's getting me.
T	(WWR)	It's getting you.
C		It's those faces.
T	(WWR)	It's those faces, ugly.
C		They're mad and black.
T	(WWR)	They're mad and black.
C		I'm drowning.
		[Cries.]
		It's only one.
T	(FR)	You're crying. You're drowning. It's only one.
C		It's smothering me. There is no water in the tub.
T	(WWR)	It's smothering you. No water.
C		No water . . . the face is smothering me.
		[C. cries more. Long pause.]
T	(WWR)	No water . . . the face is smothering you. You're crying.
C		It's my ex-wife. She is smothering me.
		[Long pause.]
		Oh, I'm in the basement.
T	(WWR)	I'm in the basement.
C		Help me.
		[C. sobs.]
T	(WWR)	It's your ex-wife.
	(RR)	You're in the basement.
C		Yeah, it's cold and dark.
T	(WWR)	It's cold and dark.
C		My bed is in the corner. It's small.
T	(WWR)	My bed is in the corner. It's small.
C		I sleep in the basement. My marriage smothered me.
T	(WWR)	My marriage smothered me.
	(FR)	You look pained, eyes big.
C		Yeah, I hurt. My marriage smothered me. It's like I was drowning in the relationship.
T	(WWR)	You're hurting, the marriage was smothering. Your relationship was like drowning.
C		All those years. I was suffocating because of our wedding

		vows. We couldn't get a divorce because we were Catholic. Being married again is being tied to those horrible memories of our marriage and religion.
T	(WWR)	Marriage is horrible because of vows.
C		I can't be married. I'm afraid of being suffocated and being lost at sea.
T	(WWR)	I can't be married. I'm afraid of being suffocated and being lost at sea.
C		It took forever for an annulment before. I can't live forever like that again.
T	(WWR)	It took forever for an annulment before. I can't live forever like that again.
T	(FR)	You stopped crying.
C		I don't know how to be married right. When I go to bed, I remember the nights in the basement. Oh God, they were horrible.

Later, Michael started dealing with issues relating to his past and current marriage. He had gained insight into how his past marriage affected his current marriage. The hallucinations ceased.

Example 4
The next example shows three crucial stages in therapeutic work with hallucinations: contact, integration, and assimilation.

In the first two stages we can see some reference to the language of Gestalt theory. Perls (1976) describes the 'Me' and 'Not Me' experience as a contact boundary. This contact boundary can be used as a point of contact between self and hallucination. With a literal contact between self and hallucination, a dramatic integration of the hallucination occurs, presenting what Polster and Polster (1974) describe as a 'contact episode', whereas in the third stage the client needs a more gradual assimilation of the experience so that it can become an aspect of the 'self-sense' (Gendlin, 1964). This can be achieved by experiential reflections (Gendlin, 1968).

Vignette

The client was a woman diagnosed as paranoid schizophrenic with homicidal and suicidal impulses. She was non-medicated and attended outpatient psychotherapy twice weekly for several years. The client had been hallucinating for several months a huge, coiled and menacing python. The python would be present in the morning when she put her feet on the floor upon arising from bed. The client related that it was present in the rear seat of her automobile as she was driving to therapy. The snake was experienced as coiled into a figure eight, lying between the client and therapist during sessions.

Developing contact

The snake was coiled between the therapist and the client. If the client moved close to the python, it would raise its head in a menacing fashion. Since the python appeared in three-dimensional space, it was mutually decided to walk around it to find a perimeter of psychological safety for the client. This process took several sessions.

The perimeter of psychological safety for the client was a half-circle that arched between the client's and therapist's chairs. This half-circle was a literal dividing line between 'psychotic space' (three-dimensional python hallucination) and 'sane space' (an area that was hallucination-free). The half-circle functioned as the contact boundary.

Contact was developed by having the client and therapist jointly walk the semi-circle together. Gradually, the client learned to develop a contact gradient. She would walk farther away from and then closer to the contact boundary half-circle. This would allow her to experiment with her experiencing. Moving closer to the contact point would produce more menacing writhing by the snake. The client would react by increased trembling, sweating, gasping, loss of bladder control — that is, terror reactions. She would also experience a fever. There was some concern for her physiological safety. This work was only possible because of the deep closeness of a person-centred relationship and the client's drive to get well.

Gradually, the client became skilled at controlling her own contact capacities. This client's autonomy and self-directedness were respected. She learned to approach the hallucination and increase her capacity to tolerate stressful feelings.

Integrative contact episode

During a mutually agreed single session, the client integrated the hallucination by making direct contact with this three-dimensional image of a python. The integration was achieved by walking with the client and approaching the half-circle contact boundary, and literally entering the psychotic (hallucinatory) space. The snake reared and sunk his teeth into the client. At this point the client screamed at the therapist: 'You betrayed me — not you too!' and proceeded to confuse me with her mother (good mother, bad mother).

I became concerned that a psychotic transference had occurred and that the client would become more psychotic and isolated from a therapeutic relationship. This did not occur. The client continued to experientially process. She reached the clarity that the snake was her homicidal mother.

Assimilation

The client slowly assimilated the meaning of the newly integrated experiences by experiential processing (Gendlin, 1968). The assimilation phase followed the contact episode almost immediately — within 24 hours. Newly integrated experiences, although viewed as real, often do not have a self-sense quality. The meaning of the newly integrated experience is not 'worked through'.

By experiential reflections (Gendlin, 1968), the client clarified the following:

- This is my psychotic split. The snake (action and parts) are my not acknowledged experiences. I retained the beautiful aspects of my mother and denied her homicide.
- I had to go crazy, not to go crazy. I had to deny being a murder object of my mother.
- The snake felt like my mother's kill wish. Now I know she really wanted to kill me.

Shortly thereafter, the hallucination shrank in size and dimension, the image relocated to between her mother's breasts, lost realism and intensity, and faded away.

Chapter 6

Newer Applications of Pre-Therapy

Hallucinatory voices

Often, during the lectures on visual hallucinations, people would ask about the application of contact reflections with auditory hallucinations. To this point, to my knowledge there has been no case material verifying this possibility. Subsequently, Jill Prouty reports working with auditory hallucinations using contact reflections within the context of a psychodrama.

In the following vignette the client was a young woman who had previously lived in a foreign country. At age 12 she was sexually abused. Her abusers told her that if she discussed them, she and her family would not be able to emigrate to the USA. During the process of a psychodrama at a mental health facility, the client reported hearing voices.

Vignette

Client		The voices.
		[Client puts hands on head.]
Therapist (BR)		Your hands are on your head.
C		*[Moves hands to cover her eyes.]*
T	(FR)	Your hands cover your eyes.
T	(BR)	You're breathing deeply.
C		*[The client removes her hands from her eyes and looks at the floor.]*
T	(SR)	You're looking at the floor.
T	(SR)	There is a green carpet in this room.
C		*[No response.]*
T	(SR)	We're standing here together.
T	(BR)	You're breathing easier now.
C		*[The client looks directly at the therapist.]*
T	(SR)	You looked directly at me.
C		*[The client puts her hands on the side of her head and then over her ears.]*

		I hear voices.
T	(WWR)	You hear voices.
C		The voice says, 'You die, you should kill yourself.'
T	(WWR)	The voice says, 'You die, you should kill yourself.'
		[Looking directly at the therapist, the client began her story about the actual abuse scene. Reality contact had been established.]
T	(RR)	You said earlier that you heard voices.

Since communicative contact about the voices had been developed by the use of Pre-Therapy the therapist then changed to classical psychodramatic technique, that is, developing the roles for the drama and setting the scene.

T	Is it one voice or many?
C	One.
T	Male or female?
C	Male. My brother.
T	Choose someone in the group to be your brother.

The therapist states:

Further evidence for Reality Contact is indicated by the client's ability to choose a group member to be in the role of her brother. As the psychodrama continued, the client was able to release her rage at her brother for his inability to protect her during the abuse. In addition, the client was able to process the guilt and anger over these feelings. These feelings were the origin of the voice saying, 'You should die, you should kill yourself'.

This vignette illustrates the use contact reflections to enable and initiate therapy, and also the use of hallucinatory voices as an access to important therapeutic material.

Multiple personality

Roy (1991, 1997) describes the use of Pre-Therapy as an adjunctive method in the treatment of multiple personality disorder. According to Roy, such clients often experience personality fragments on the margin of, or completely removed from, consciousness. These personality fragments often lack experiential felt-sense and may be expressed in halting and primitive symbolisations. For example, a client would express singular words such as 'face', 'window', 'cellar door', 'bleeding', etc. which Roy would reflect through word-for-word responses. Roy goes on to describe a Facial Reflection, 'You look angry'. According to the client, this helped make contact with important angry feelings embodied in her face, of which she was previously unaware. Roy further states, 'Dissociated material, whether it is as distinctive as a separate personality, or much less so, must be experienced and "allowed to live in the world"'. Working with the same client, several years later, Roy describes a full session utilising contact reflections to integrate an alternate self and dissociated memories.

Profoundly retarded

McWilliams (1996) reports the application of contact reflections with a non-verbal profoundly retarded young woman. The contact work was supplied by her stepmother. The stepmother used body reflections involving finger, head and arm movements, as well as non-verbal sounds. She would also reflect facial expressions such as happiness. All these were combined with the principle of reiteration. This contact work was woven into daily living rather than as a therapeutic session. Positive results for the client included a sharp increase in contact with the world, self and others. Her increased contact with her world, was evidenced through her attention to surrounding, situations. Her contact with the other was expressed through her being less isolated, being more present with her father and increased family mutuality. Her improved contact with herself was evidenced in a shift from a non-responsive mode of seeing herself in the mirror, to a smiling, satisfied mode of looking. The net result of contact was a decrease in psychological isolation and an increase in psychological presence.

A pre-vocational workshop for the profoundly handicapped reports the application of Pre-Therapy as a 'recreational' method incorporated into their programmatic schedule. They describe the application of contact reflections combined with a playful attitude; the intent being 'play' and 'entertainment'.

Social autism

At the suggestion of Dr. Henrietta Morato of the University of Sao Paulo, Brazil, Pre-Therapy may have relevance for children who are culturally deprived or 'socially autistic'. These children have diminished psychological contact due to their poverty-connected trauma. As native populations migrate to densely populated urban centres, family stress and disorganisation increasingly occur. These events often end in loss of the sense of self and, in some cases, a withdrawal from reality itself.

Chapter 7

Further Thoughts

Through further reflection I have observed some common threads in the work of other thinkers and points that touch upon other theoretical articulations. These came together for me forming a further 'kaleidoscope of meaning'.

Rogers

Pre-Therapy has its roots in Client-Centred Therapy; the famed 'attitudes' or 'conditions' play an important and prominent role in the application of contact reflections. It is inconceivable that such therapeutic work could be practised without them. It is very clear that unconditional positive regard and empathy must be present in a highly congruent manner. They function as necessary co-elements with contact in the therapeutic causal chain.

However, to think of Pre-Therapy as only a new method of conveying the 'attitudes' is to omit the gains derived from expanding and further developing the concept of psychological contact. These gains are both practical and theoretical. First, practically, the contact reflections make concrete the attitudes for clients formerly not able to receive them. And second, the contact reflections also make contact between therapist and client occur where there was none or minimum amounts.

That is the additional practical power of Pre-Therapy. The theoretical strength of Pre-Therapy lies in the identification of valid constructs (Reality, Affect, Communication, see pp. 17–18) thereby adding new dimensions to the Client-Centred Approach. In summary it must be said that the development of the theory of contact is an evolution in client-centred thought that combines the attitudes and contact — both necessary to each other when working with low-functioning clients (those who are mentally ill, or with the diagnosis schizophrenia, or who have developmental disabilities or some aspects of dissociation).

Lacan

The French psychoanalyst, Lacan, stands very far-removed from the client-centred and phenomenological way of understanding. Nevertheless, through him, an important developmental perspective may be opened for Pre-Therapy. Lacan (1977) speaks of a 'Mirror Stage of Development' based on comparable observations of human children and apes. Lacan had noticed that six-month-old human babies react to their own reflection. Young apes, on the other hand, did not. From this he deduced a specific level of human development, the 'mirror stage'. It was seen as an important aspect of 'I-development' or self-identification.

Based upon observations of a profoundly retarded woman, I was able to literally see the movement from non-recognition to self-recognition in a mirror. The consequences of Pre-Therapy treatment paralelled the developmental observations of Lacan.

Minkowski

Eugene Minkowski, a phenomenological psychiatrist and pioneer in the description of schizophrenic experience, is likewise important for me. He describes the 'loss of vital contact' between the person and reality as the earmark of schizophrenia (Minkowski, 1970). This is a clear parallel to the concept of Pre-Therapy, which views 'empathic contact' as the deciding factor in establishing the therapeutic process for chronic schizophrenic clients. My description of the treatment (empathic contact) is identifiable in his definition of the problem (lack of vital contact).

R.D. Laing

I found powerful parallels in R. D. Laing's radical existential–phenomenological approach to schizophrenia. During my entire teaching period (1970–1995) I used Laing's book, *The Divided Self*, as a foundation for teaching the phenomenological approach with schizophrenic patients. The title especially linked with my view, that the hallucination reveals within itself a deeply torn self-structure — a divided self.

The term 'Disembodied Self' used by Laing captures exactly my experience of the hallucination as an experience as 'outside one's own body' This was important to me theoretically, since it helped me to clearly differentiate pre-symbolic hallucinatory experiencing from the concrete bodily-felt experiencing process of Gendlin.

Perls

Fritz Perls' concept of 'Contact as an Ego Function' (Perls, 1969) made possible my own position of Reality, Affective and Communicative Contact as client psychological processes. Perls' way of looking at the dream as a self-fragment (Polster and Polster, 1974) enabled me to view hallucinations as a fragment of the self.

Freud

Unlike Freud, who had described both dreams and hallucinations similarly as 'Primary Process', I see a phenomenological difference between a dream and an hallucination. The dream is 'my dream' and 'I had it last night' — it is something experienced, which plays itself out, within the boundaries of self. The hallucination is disconnected — it becomes experienced as not belonging to self, rather as objective external reality. Therefore, in contrast to a dream, which Freud described as 'projection' (within the self-boundary); I describe the hallucination as 'extrojection' (outside the self-boundary).

Analogous to Freud, who viewed the dream as the 'royal road to the unconscious', I view the hallucination as the 'royal road to the unconscious'.

Rogers and hallucinations

In client-centred terms, one could describe the psychological division between hallucination and self as the 'greatest possible incongruence between self and experience'(Rogers, 1961). In contrast to this stands the description of Rogers' 'fully-functioning person' as the 'greatest possible congruence between self and experience.' The two opposite modes of experiencing exist — the hallucinating person is completely closed to self-experience, while the 'fully functioning person' is very open to self-experience.

In conclusion

I want my theoretical 'round trip' to end with Carl Rogers. All theoretical and methodological evolutions remain rooted in the therapeutic relationship as Rogers defined it. We cannot lose sight of this. It has been a long journey from the origins of Pre-Therapy rooted in my family experience, to the point of multifaceted theoretical connections with other authors.

That Pre-Therapy is being further developed by colleagues in different parts of the world, is an endorsement which gives me comfort and courage. My deepest hope is that Pre-Therapy opens up a new way of understanding psychosis and thus carries forward the tradition of taking psychotic behaviour and meaning seriously. This approach is offered to suffering people to bring them help. I hope that the concept of Pre-Symbolic Experiencing carries with it the therapeutic value of hallucinations and that this will become more recognised and utilised.

For the future, I wish that Pre-Therapy becomes integrated as an extension and widening of client-centred theory that makes it possible to work in meaningful ways with trauma and personality splits. I hope that Pre-Therapy not only becomes used as an individual process, but also as a useful therapeutic model in the care of the elderly and people with severe mental impairments. With this in mind, my European colleagues developed concepts and guidelines which are described in the following sections of this book.

Part 1 References

Arieti, S. (1955) *Interpretation of Schizophrenia*. New York: Robert Brunner.

Binswanger, L. (1958) *Existence: A New Dimension in Psychiatry and Psychology* (p. 194). New York: Basic Books.

Boss, M. (1963) *Psychoanalysis and Daseinsanalysis*. New York: Basic Books, pp. 5–27.

Boss, M. (1980) Personal communication.

Buber, M. (1964) Elements of the interhuman. In: M. Friedman (Ed.), *The World of Existentialism*. New York: Random House, pp. 229, 547.

Cassirer, F. (1955) Man: An animal symbolicum. In: D. Runes (Ed.) *Treasury of Philosophy*. New York: Philosophical Library, pp. 227–9.

De Vre, R. (1992) *Prouty's Pre-Therapie*. Gent: Lizenziatsarbeit, Psychologische Fakultat der Universitat Gent.

Dinacci, A. (1994) Colloqulo Pre-Terapeutico: Criterio obiettivo di valutazione. In *LEGGE e PSYCHE*, Rivista di Psicologia Giuridica, Anno III, Nr. 1

Dinacci, A. (1995) Experimental Research on the Psychological Treatment of Schizophrenic Clients with Garry Prouty's Pre-Therapy and Innovative Developments. Vortrag, gehalten bei der 3rd ICCCEP Conference, Gmunden.

Dinacci, A. (1997) Ricerca sperimentale sul trattamento psicologico dei pazienti schizophrenici con la pre-terapia di Dr. G. Prouty. In: *Psicologia della persona*, II (4).

Farber, M. (1959) *Naturalism and Subjectivism*. Albany, NY: State University of New York Press, p. 87.

Farber, M. (1967) *Phenomenology and Existence: Towards a Philosophy within Nature*. Albany, NY: State University of New York Press, pp. 14–37.

Gendlin, F. T. (1964) A theory of personality change. In: P. Worchel and D. Byrne (Eds.) *Personality Change*. New York: Grune and Stratton, pp. 102–48.

Gendlin, F. T. (1968) The experiential response. In: E. Hammer (Ed.) *Use of Interpretation in Treatment*. New York: Grune and Stratton, pp. 208–28.

Gurswitch, A. (1966) Gelb-Goldstein's concept of concrete and categorical attitude and the phenomenology of ideation. In: J. Wild (Ed.) *Studies in Phenomenology and Psychology*. Evanston, IL: Northwestern University Press, pp. 359–89.

Havens, L. (1962) The placement and movement of hallucinations in space, phenomenology and theory. *International Journal of Psychoanalysis, 43*, 426–35.

Hinterkopf, E., Prouty, G., and Brunswick, L. (1979) A pilot study of PreTherapy method applied to chronic schizophrenic patients. *Psychosocial Rehabilitation Journal, 3*, 11–19.

Husserl, E. (1977) *Phenomenological Psychology: Lectures, Sommer 1925.* Den Haag: Martinus Nijhoff.

Jaspers, K. (1963) *General Psychopathology.* Manchester: Manchester University Press, p. 55.

Jaspers, K. (1971) *Philosophy,* Vol. 3. Chicago: University of Chicago Press.

Lacan, J. (1977) *Ecrits: A Selection.* New York: W. W. Norton Co, pp. 1–7.

Laing, R. D. (1969) *The Divided Self.* New York: Pantheon Books.

Langer, S. K. (1961) *Philosophy in a New Key.* New York: Mentor Books.

Mahrer, A. (1992) Discovery oriented psychotherapy research: Rationale, aims and methods. In: R. B. Miller (Ed.) *The Restoration of Dialogue: Readings in the Philosophy of Clinical Psychology.* Washington, DC: American Psychological Association, pp. 570–84.

May, R. (1983) *The Discovery of Being.* New York: W. W. Norton Co, p. 153.

McWilliams, K. (1996) Life Enrichment of a Profoundly Retarded Woman. Vortrag am Pre-Therapy Training Seminar, Osteopathic Hospital, Chicago IL.

Merleau-Ponty, M. (1962) The phenomenal field. In: T. Honderich (Ed.): *The Phenomenology of Perception.* London: Routledge and Kegan Paul, p. 60.

Minkowski, E. (1970) Schizophrenia. In: J. Wild (Hrsg.): *Lived Time.* Evanston, IL: Northwestern University Press, pp. 281–2.

Passons, W. R. (1975) *Gestalt Approaches in Counseling.* New York: Holt, Rinehart and Winston, p. 100.

Perls, F. S. (1969) The ego as a function of the organism. *Ego, Hunger and Aggression.* New York: Vintage Books, p. 139.

Perls, F. S. (1976) *The Gestalt Approach and Eyewitness to Therapy.* New York: Bantam.

Polster, E. and Polster, M. (1974) *Gestalt Therapy Integrated.* New York: Vintage Books.

Prouty, G. (1966) Psychotherapy with a psychotic retardate. Unpublished audiotape, J. P. Kennedy School for Exceptional Children, Palos Park, Illinois.

Prouty, G. (1977) Protosymbolic method: A phenomenological treatment of schizophrenics. *Journal of Mental Imagery, 1* (2), 339–42.

Prouty, G. (1983) Hallucinatory contact: A phenomenological treatment of schizophrenics. *Journal of Communication Therapy, 2* (1), 99–103.

Prouty, G. (1986) The pre-symbolic structure and therapeutic transformation of hallucinations. In: M. Wolpin, J. Shorr and L. Kreuger (Eds.) *Imagery, 4.* New York: Plenum Press, pp. 99–106.

Prouty, G. (1990) Pre-Therapy: A theoretical evolution in the person-centered/experiential psychotherapy of schizophrenia and retardation. In: G. Lietaer,

J. Rombauts and R. Van Balen (Eds.) *Client-Centered and Experiential Psychotherapy in the Nineties.* Leuven: Leuven University Press, pp. 645–58.

Prouty, G. (1991) The pre-symbolic structure and processing of schizophrenic hallucinations. In: L. Fusek (Ed.): *New Directions in Client-Centered Therapy: Practice with Difficult Client Populations.* Chicago: Chicago Counseling and Psychotherapy Research Center, pp. 1–18.

Prouty, G. (1994) *Theoretical Evolutions in Person-Centered/Experiential Therapy: Applications to schizophrenic and retarded psychoses.* Westport, CN: Praeger.

Prouty, G. (1997) Pre-Therapy and pre-symbolic experiencing: Evolutions in Person-Centered/Experiential approaches to psychotic and retarded experience. In: L. Greenberg, G. Lietaer and J. Watson (Eds.): *Experiential Psychotherapy: Different Perspectives.* New York: Guilford Press.

Prouty, G. and Cronwall, M. (1990) Psychotherapy with a depressed mentally retarded adult: An application of pre-therapy. In: A. Dosen and F. Menolascino, (Eds.) *Depression in Mentally Retarded Children and Adults.* Leiden: Logan Publications, pp. 281–93.

Prouty, G. and Kubiak, M. (1988a): The development of communicative contact with a catatonic schizophrenic. *Journal of Communication Therapy, 4* (1), 13–20.

Prouty, G. and Kubiak, M. (1988b) Pre-Therapy with mentally retarded/psychotic clients. *Psychiatric Aspects of Mental Retardation Reviews, 7* (10), 62–6.

Prouty, G. and Pietrzak, S. (1988) Pre-therapy method applied to persons experiencing hallucinatory images. *Person-Centered Review, 3* (4), 95–103.

Rogers, C. (1957) The necessary and sufficient conditions of therapeutic personality change. *Journal of Consulting Psychology, 21* (2), 95–103.

Rogers, C. (1959) A theory of therapy, personality and interpersonal relationships as developed in the client-centered framework. In: E. Koch (Ed.): *Psychology: A study of a science, 3* (5), 251. New York: McGraw-Hill.

Rogers, C. (1961) *On Becoming a Person.* Boston: Houghton Mifflin.

Rogers, C. (1978) The formative tendency. *Journal of Humanistic Psychology, 18,* 23–6.

Roy, B. C. (1991) A client-centered approach to multiple personality and dissociative process. In: L. Fusek (Ed.): *New Directions in Client-Centered Therapy: Practice with difficult client populations.* Chicago: Chicago Counseling and Psychotherapy Research Center, pp. 18–40.

Roy, B. C. (1997) An illustration of memory retrieval with a DID client. Presentation at the Eastern Psychological Association, Washington, DC.

Sartre, J.-P. (1956) *Being and Nothingness* New York: Washington Square Press.

Scheler, M. (1953) Phenomenology and the theory of cognition. In: *Selected Philosophical Essays.* Evanston, IL: Northwestern University Press.

Szasz, T. S. (1961) *The Myth of Mental Illness: Foundations of a theory of personal conduct.* New York: Paul B. Hoeber.

Van Werde, D. (1994) Dealing with the possibility of psychotic content in a seemingly congruent communication. In: D. Mearns (Ed.) *Developing Person-*

Centred Counselling. London: Sage Publications, pp. 125–8.

Watson, N. (1984) The empirical status of Rogers' hypothesis of the necessary and sufficient conditions for effective psychotherapy In: R. Levant and J. Shlien (Eds.) *Client-Centered Psychotherapy and the Person-Centered Approach*. New York: Praeger, pp. 17–40.

Whitehead, A. N. (1927) *Symbolism*. New York: Capricorn Books.

Part 2

Dion Van Werde

Pre-Therapy Applied on a Psychiatric Ward

Introduction

This section will illustrate how Pre-Therapy can be useful in designing a ward regime; the application of which is designed for treating psychotic patients in a residential psychiatric hospital. It is meant to inspire and to challenge readers from different backgrounds and to confront their own thinking and practice.

The relevance of my work is not limited to this specific population, but lies in the fact that it is transferrable to other settings, other populations, and other organisational demands. I am not only interested in presenting you with a particular setting for Pre-Therapy but also in showing you the process of thinking involved when implementing such an approach. I have good reasons to believe that Pre-Therapy can be inspiring and useful for other people working with other kinds of low-contact-functioning people too.

It is no easy task to present this kind of work. In general, when speaking about Pre-Therapy, and especially when reflections are written down, they tend to look simplistic, mechanical and a mere act of repeating. Beautiful moments of delicate interaction, receptiveness for the existential situation, the necessary discipline and concentration, and the relatively distant playfulness combined with a sincere and close compassion are hard to transfer on to paper. The poetry and the art tend to get lost. Therefore I recommend that readers, wherever possible, combine the reading of this book with exposure to Pre-Therapy done by experienced therapists who have had their training at the Pre-Therapy Institute, or Institute staff members, either directly, in a workshop-setting or on video-tape (e.g. Van Werde and Willemaers, 1992) and to exchange thoughts and experiences.

It is many years since we started a ward inspired by Prouty's Pre-Therapy. It began with a conference in our hospital with Garry Prouty talking about Pre-Therapy and his pre-symbolic thinking. Now, many years later, our hospital continues its support and hosts the newly formed European Pre Therapy Training Institute. It has been a long journey which has sometimes been a lonely enterprise in the sense that it was pioneering. Not only did I have to develop personally and change my work in order to accommodate Pre-Therapy, but also the thinking on the ward had to be sharpened and the relevance for everybody in the programme had to be made clear. This has been a growth process and still is.

Then there was of course the institution itself. A lot of conservative forces were at work which made it necessary to also invest time and energy in 'contact-work' with the managers. We had to create a secure space in the organisational structure in which to develop the work. In an early phase one third of my energy went directly to the patients, another third went to developing the philosophical and theoretical thinking and in educating and supervising staff and the final third in working with the institution.

In this section, you will find hard evidence for the efficacy of the approach. No statistics are presented though and the case studies have to be called case illustrations rather than n=1 research. We hope to come up with scientific data in the future, if time, money and scientific back-up is sufficiently available.

So, what is the status of what you are going to read then? I call it touchstone material — it is a report of our daily work on the ward and of our pioneering struggle to design a therapeutic approach by implementing an inspiring theory and practice.

Chapter 1

Mission Statements

The importance of being rooted

The image of the tree

When somebody is admitted to our unit, most of the time the psychotic problems and the associated suffering are obvious. As a first response, we long to relieve all the suffering, and the quicker the better. Experience however shows that these good intentions are hard to realise. Sometimes the problems are so severe and consequently the feelings of helplessness so big that we have to let go of our aspirations and learn a lesson of humility.

A first step is 'just' to accept that what we see is what we get, and that even the person suffering is an eyewitness to the whole event rather than an active participant/player. Thinking this way, some of the philosophy we work from is implied. I came to discover this philosophy better myself by working with parents and relatives of admitted people. They suffer the same helplessness and are at least as motivated to try to remove the suffering as we are. In a first contact (if asked for), the only advice we can give, the only practical hint we can offer, is that maybe accepting the fact that their relative is in the grip of a psychosis is the first necessary step in the process of dealing with the suffering. Everything else comes later.

In our conceptualisation of psychosis, we however don't automatically see the psychotic symptomatology as the main problem. The real difficulty lies in ascertaining the balance between healthy and problematic functioning. This implies that we always presuppose a healthy part in the person we are dealing with, a core that can be reached and can be strengthened, however relatively small it may be. For us, there is always somebody we can address!

When talking about all this to the clients and their friends and relations, we present the image of the tree. The upper part, the top (branches, leaves, etc.) represents everything that is in the air, meaning things like thoughts, dreams, daydreaming, nightmares, delusions, hallucinations of any mode, even clairvoyance and extra-sensory perceptions of any kind and so on. The lower part (roots) represents everything that is grounded, rooted, solid, firm and offering foundations. We associate the latter with things like healthy food, a good balance between night (being asleep) and day (being awake), constructive social contacts, physical health, a balance between work and leisure activities, careful grooming and so on.

When reasoning further along the lines of our image, we would say that it is essential that there is a balance between the upper and the lower parts of the tree. More specifically, if you have a large top to carry, you also need a vast bed of roots. Psychotic people are victims of their thoughts, fantasies, delusions and so on. They are overwhelmed by them and are in shortage of firm ground under their feet. They often don't sleep any more, their feeding habits and grooming habits deteriorate, they retreat from social contact. As caregivers, we tend to be exclusively attentive to psychotic symptomatology. But conversely we have experienced the relevance of also working on the restoration and strengthening of a patient's contact functions in order to prepare for eventually addressing psychotic content later. We explain to people that when you have poor or inadequate roots, it only takes a small wind to blow your tree down. It's not so much the vast top that is the problem, but the poor anchorage.

Certainly seen from a therapeutic point of view, this represents a positive image of humans and raises not only hope but also some pointers if one considers engaging in a therapeutic journey.

About the roots

Sometimes, as 'healthy' persons, we may have experienced strange things ourselves. Who isn't familiar with the phenomenon of hearing one's own name called in the street? If rendered curious, maybe even rendered suspicious to the point of checking out where the call came from and who was yelling, one discovers that it was a misunderstanding, that the sound was similar, but not a name at all or maybe that it indeed was a name like one's own, but that it was meant for somebody else. For a split second, we have had the opportunity to realise what it can mean to live in a world that is continuously filled with such 'misunderstandings'. A 'healthy' person can easily use their common sense without losing control or without becoming flooded by this kind of singular and time-limited experience. We can say that such a person, notwithstanding a possible moment of existential doubt, manages to stay rooted in everyday reality, in the world as 'we' know it, in the 'shared' reality. Hearing one's name called is a relatively easy situation. What about hearing it during the night, disturbing your sleep and starting off a circle of anxiety and restlessness that provokes even more auditory turmoil? What if the calling is very loud and hostile? What if it happens during a quarrel with your husband or at a party where you are supposed to welcome the guests? Numerous examples of such contact-endangering experiences can be given. The point is always: are you rooted enough to balance these experiences with healthy functioning? Can your system of roots carry such a vast top? If not, is it a momentary and occasional problem (not slept enough, on drugs, in an emotional episode) or is it a structural one, meaning that you are bound to collapse since your level of psychological resources is so low that any extra stress will trigger off more psychotic experiencing anyhow?

From this you can see that we are not automatically in favour of instantly and iatrogenically cutting off the top of the tree when people seek help. At best, we see these kinds of interventions as an attempt to manage the problematic situation. In a medical setting and within the limitations of the system (number of personnel, responsibilities of taking care for 20 'beds', and so on), the compromise is made to use drugs since the resources for offering therapeutic relationships are limited. Who are we to say that the latter would always be sufficiently therapeutic anyhow? So, when somebody, for example, hears voices, we try to engage with this client in a relationship so that we can find out together what the problem is, how a workable distance towards the problem can be reached, what the most urgent thing to do is and how the future needs to be planned.

About the top of the tree

Of course, if the patient wants to, he can be freed from psychotic symptomatology relatively easily. Medication or electro-convulsive therapy can do the job. The price to be paid for such treatment is almost always a severe cutting of the top of the tree and the loss of inherent life quality that could be drawn from it. This ties up with Prouty's notion of pre-expressive functioning. Psychotic behaviour is seen as meaningful, as a way of dealing with something and a way of expressing, without however reaching the communicative standards that are required for congruent communication. Nevertheless, if one ignores, denies, neglects or doesn't listen carefully to these ways of functioning, one underestimates their power in the psychotherapeutic process. As Prouty describes theoretically and illustrates with case examples, the hallucination can be the royal road to the unconscious (Prouty, 1994, p. 88). Prouty documents several cases of visual hallucinations that were processed to the core experience, which proved to be the originating point of these hallucinations. Not many of us, I believe, have accomplished this kind of therapy. For me, it has to do with the level of congruence of the therapist. People suffering psychosis are particularly skilled at knowing from a distance the difference between those who are rooted enough in themselves, sincere and really containing, and those who are going to play tricks on them. Only if the conditions are optimal, I think, do people dare to take the risk of really looking at their experiences, especially when these are so private, delicate and anxiety-provoking as are those experiences that are proven to be generators of psychosis.

The treatment of choice is to contact and work with that part of a person that is still rooted and operative and to ally with that part that can congruently deal with the situation or that still has some strength left. As psychotherapists or contact facilitators, we try to make contact with that, accompany it, strengthen the anchorage and help the person gradually to master the situation again. If our clients can join us in the image of the tree, this means that a certain distance towards their psychotic functioning is already established. 'You are looking at your problem.' 'You' doesn't equal 'problem' anymore. This is an excellent starting point for further therapy. Or 'you' and 'the problem' start a dialogue, and what was overwhelming is now listened to and maybe reveals its encoded messages. Or maybe the therapist is allowed to become an ally of the 'you' of the patient and perhaps in a 'trialogue' between patient, therapist and 'problems', things that can be worked out. Maybe, and probably only very gradually, clients can become themselves again, decoding and integrating their psychotic experiencing. What we say to people however is that extremes need to be balanced and that everyone needs to find out for themselves how strong they are, what the therapeutic priorities for the moment are and how vast a top can be carried with the given roots.

In Figure 1 we present a handout that we use during the partner and family evenings that we regularly organise. It helps us to explain and illustrate the way we work. When we go from this to the overall concept of anchorage and the idea that we regard contact as defined by Prouty as an antidote for psychotic suffering, parents and partners of patients feel themselves and their relatives very much understood!

Figure 1: The image of the tree

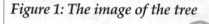

TOP
- clairvoyance
- hallucinatory perceptions
- delusional thinking
- experiences due to intoxication, organic diseases, depression, shock, anxiety attacks, stress
- being over-fatigued
- dreaming
- worrying
- daydreaming
- fantasising

ROOTS	**ANCHORING WARDWORK** by
• physical health and well-being	• GP, psychiatrist, nurses
• a place in society (economical juridical, administrative, family)	• social worker
• living in a group (neighbourhood, family, work, school)	• being in a ward setting, group activities
• healthy day–night rhythm	• ward's house rules
• healthy food	• hospital kitchen or preparing own meals on the ward
• groomed and active body	• movement therapy
• constructive social contacts	• groupwork, communication exercises, activities 'outside'
• a balance between work and leisure	• therapies versus free-time on the ward
• working with material	• labour therapy, housekeeping tasks
• contact with the affective self	• individual contacts with psychologist, nurses

Applied phenomenology

What are the qualities that we find essential in our work? Can we find some kind of overall belief statement that is simple and powerful enough to summarise everything that we believe in and think of as being important when working as a caregiver with clients suffering a process of profound incongruence? Chris Deleu, a close colleague of mine who also works on the ward, and myself came to an answer by discussing in detail how we work and what we find important. This process took several years. This question was particularly challenging because Chris, as the psychologist responsible for the perception-training group (see *Perception-training group*, p. 97), focuses on working with everyday reality, and as an individual therapist, I work a lot with psychotic material. Nevertheless, Chris and myself have much in common. Of course, our person-centred background explains a lot, but then what about Chris doing exercises with the patients like exactly copying a stone or carefully listening to surrounding sounds? And what is the link with me reflecting unintelligible words and body posture? We discovered that a phenomenological attitude is the common base of our work, whether it is in everyday realities or in highly private, so-called psychotic, experiences.

When we really want people or things to disclose themselves, approaching them is best done by leaving aside entire previous knowledge and tendency for instant judgement. It is necessary to let the other person, the thing or events under observation speak for themselves. You are not allowed to take, but you are invited to give and to receive. This is saying 'yes' to everything that wants to show itself. It is submitting yourself to the facts.

When we approach a thing or a person without prejudices, we then can be emotionally moved by the object of our perception. Therefore, we must let go of existing feelings of sympathy and antipathy for that particular object. We need to be pure so that we can be really open and can be inwardly touched. This way of surrendering to the facts is how we understand phenomenology. This is what we recognise as a cornerstone of everything we believe in and practise.

I will now give three short examples to illustrate how this attitude is applied in the daily work of Chris and myself. Illustrations one and two come from different ongoing verbal psychotherapies. When the client reports on his hallucinatory image, or on a disturbing noise, the described attitude is clearly visible. The client is invited to stand still and look at what announces itself. Chris and I use a complementary method though. In the first case, Pre-Therapy inspiration is used to address the psychotic content. In the second example, the client is invited to do a listening exercise and to direct her phenomenological attention to the surrounding reality. In both cases something therapeutic happens, as a result of the described way of listening and exercising. The third illustration breathes the same phenomenological atmosphere and again illustrates the attitude of being quiet and listening — if it is to a piece of nature that was visited several times (see also Deleu and Van Werde, 1998). As a careful and attentive reader, you will discover that the supposed contradiction between working with idiosyncratic psychotic reality versus working or exercising with the outer and shared reality is synthetically overcome by the use of that described phenomenological attitude. The therapist 'chooses' a target (the surrounding sounds in Illustration 2) or a target presents itself (the woman in white in Illustration 1 and the mushrooms in Illustration 3). They are handled in quite the same manner — call it respectful, call it phenomenological, call it 'in poverty', 'obedient' and 'pure'. Out of genuine interest, the object under observation is questioned on a very concrete level, without interpreting, judging or evaluating. By doing so, it really is invited to disclose itself.

Illustration 1
'I want to return to my wife'

This vignette comes from a session with Dennis (D), a borderline-psychotic young man. The therapist (T) and D know each other well and, up to this point in the session, communication has been on a congruent level. It is near the end of the calendar year . . .

T		**D, is there something you wish for next year? You don't have to say it if you don't want to, of course . . .**
D		**Yes, I want to go back to my wife.**
		[With a big smile, moist eyes and looking very happy.]
T		*[Perplexed because T knows that there is no woman at all in D's life at the moment, and is touched by this New Year's wish.]*
	(FR)	**We are about to cry the two of us!**
		[And in saying this, also indicating his own wet eyes . . .]
D		*[Keeps smiling and is obviously enjoying the idea of a meeting with his wife and its quality.]*
T	(WWR)	**You want to return to your wife.**
		[Reflecting word for word and psychologically fully present at that imagined and experienced reunion].
D		*[Stares at a point to the side of T.]*
T	(BR)	*[Points at the place that D is addressing — by doing so, accepting client's reality — and asks]*
		Do you see her?
		[T wants to inform himself about the sense impressions of what the client perceives as a way of making contact. This contact may reveal or accompany emotions that can be reflected in their turn, so that both the image and the affect can begin to develop. During a previous conversation, D had also perceived his loved one. She was dressed in shiny white, with gloves on her feet (sic) and she invited him to return to a hospital where he had been before. She had also promised that she would be waiting for him...]
D		*[Nods his head affirmatively.]*

		Yes.
T		**Is she in white?**
		[Again referring to previous information.]
D		**No, in colour.**
T		**Is she saying something?**
		[The therapist afterwards regrets that he changed the topic to a different sense field. Probably it would have been better to stay closer to the given and asked more about the colours.]
D		**No.**
T	(FR)	*[Meanwhile staring more and more and then looking at T. D holds his eyes and looks at T.]*
		You look surprised.
D		*[Nods his head.]*
		Yes.
		[. . . and obviously contacts his feelings: affective contact.]
T	(BR)	**You nod 'yes'.**
	(RR)	**Just a while ago, you looked over here…**
		[. . . and points again at that hallucinatory place beside him . . .]
	(SR)	**…and now you're looking at me.**
D		*[Nods affirmatively. D keeps looking at T so does not follow the pointing at the place of the hallucination – and looks as if he himself is surprised that such a thing as a hallucination has occurred. He clearly doesn't know how to handle it and seems willing to try anything to keep his eyes grounded in reality.]*
T	(BR)	*[Also nods his head – as a way of communicating his understanding.]*
		. . .
D		**Can I go upstairs?**
T		*[T interprets this as a congruent request and implicitly agrees to stop and to let the psychotic content drop. Probably continuation would have endangered the newly regained contact with reality and with the affective state.]*
		OK, I'll walk you to the ward.

Illustration 2
'A deafening noise'

During one of our conversations, in which Agnes is once more upset by a disturbing noise, I propose a short listening exercise. I invite her to listen actively to sounds she can distinguish in her surroundings, starting with those close by and then moving away to the most remote one and to return 'the same way'. She does the exercise in silence and reports afterwards that to her surprise the deafening noise hadn't been present during the exercise.

The patient had made a journey in space (from close by to further away and back) and in time (one step after the other). Doing so, she was able to identify sounds and could afterwards describe their different qualities: the sound of the barking dog far away, steps in the room above our heads, the roaring sound of a jet flying over and so on. The point, however, was not that she could name the sounds, but that she was able to register the different qualities of what she perceived. This small exercise taught Agnes that she herself, at least temporarily, could monitor/direct her attention and by doing so, master — if even temporarily — the disturbing sounds that she thought uncontrollable.

Although these kinds of exercises are beneficial for training attention and concentration (the patient aims her attention at, in this case, audible phenomena), the basic attitude is crucial: to listen quietly in a receptive manner.

Illustration 3
October, month of the mushrooms

Each year in September or October, the wood in our grounds is full of mushrooms that grow on fallen trees and cut wood. Each year during this period we make the same walk every Friday afternoon and do observation exercises. The first week we mainly pay attention to where the mushrooms grow, what they look like, how they smell, taste and feel. Different senses are addressed. Every participant can stop the group when he or she runs into something interesting. During the second and third week the attention automatically shifts to how the mushrooms are changing in form, colours, sizes and so on. The basic attitude is again a phenomenological one and can be summarised as being quiet and 'listening'. The effect of these walks is remarkable and contrary to the so-called 'negative' symptoms of psychosis and other forms of alienation (see Van Werde and Van Akoleyen, 1994). Participants become expectant and attentive to new and changing things. Not infrequently, people experience joy and feel encouraged since their own will power is being addressed.

The thread running through these illustrations — others could be given — is the translation of a phenomenological attitude into the daily practice of how a therapist or client can work with material that presents or announces itself, whether it's a hallucination, a disturbing sound or something in the natural environment. In practice, we continuously have to choose between reflecting and offering opportunities to engage with (the shared) reality. The first illustration especially shows that in daily practice the two are interwoven. When the patient shows his psychosis, the therapist consequently shifts back to pre-expressive interaction and starts to use Pre-Therapy reflections. When the patient reports on his hallucinatory image, they both pause and start to question this phenomenon: yes, he sees her; no, she is not dressed in white but in colour; she doesn't speak and so on. It means questioning the perceptual qualities of what presents itself, from a welcoming attitude. This way of working, which combines reflecting and questioning and finds its synthesis in the phenomenological attitude, bridges the supposed contradiction between 'being with' and 'doing with' the client (see also the next section) for our next mission statement, about being person-centred and active). It fosters therapeutic process and − if applied on a large scale − establishes a contact milieu (cf. Van Werde 1995).

In our illustrations, the immediate impact of the use of the phenomenological method was limited though significant: Dennis, who shares his hallucination with the therapist, contacts his astonishment (affective contact). He is empowered to choose whether or not he is willing to explore his hallucination. He prefers not to, protects himself from becoming flooded and returns to the ward. In the second illustration, the woman succeeds in putting aside the disturbing noise through responding to the therapist's suggestion to do a listening exercise and through the anchorage that subsequently follows. Maybe this will prove to be the first step of a therapeutic process that will lead her to master, or even to decode or understand, the deafening noise. The mushrooms in our third illustration are first spotted, then exactly described and investigated by means of a welcoming, observing and listening attitude. A shuttle between looking and seeing arises and different feelings can be tapped into and expanded.

To move between 'contacting' and 'revealing' is essential. We are receptive to what's coming, go towards it and, by our attitude, invite it to disclose itself. As Goethe said: 'You can only know the things you love'. We call it applied phenomenology − not unknown in Person-Centred Therapy. Rogers (1966), Gendlin (1968) and Prouty (1994) are our historical reference points.

Finally, it is our view that both Pre-Therapy (Illustration 1) and observation training (Illustrations 2 and 3) are aimed at awakening and mobilising clients' own proactive forces. Medication that deadens or exhausts these forces needs to be used in a restricted, limited way, if used at all. We consider that the development and use of medication that is free of this kind of (iatrogenic) negative side-effects would be an important contribution by the medico-pharmaceutical world to the realisation of holistic phenomenological healthcare.

Being person-centred and 'active': practical evolutions in Person-Centred/Experiential Therapy

Under this heading, I would like to say something about two evolution lines that cross-sect and that are both of importance in understanding our daily work on the ward. First is the line of the historical evolution of Person-Centred Therapy, and second is the line connected to the necessities of being in a ward setting and working with a multidisciplinary team.

History of Person-Centred Therapy
Although Person-Centred Therapy has always put the accent on the relationship, a lot has changed in the meaning of that relationship. In 1990, Germain Lietaer reports in his book *Client-Centred and Experiential Psychotherapy*

in the Nineties on how he thinks client-centred therapy has been practised in the 1970s and 1980s. He points out how more and more person-centred therapists permit themselves certain directivity in their work.

Most client-centred therapists no longer feel uneasy when defining their work as an active influencing process in which they try to stimulate the unfolding of the client's experiencing process through task-oriented interventions. As 'process experts' they have found a way to intervene actively without falling into manipulation or authoritarian control. In addition, there is a tendency to describe in more detail the specific interventions of the therapist with each type of client, in each type of setting, for each type of ongoing process, etc. Rogers has always restricted himself to the description of what he found essential, the 'heart of the matter'. He left it to every therapist to give it its concrete form and thus certainly respected everybody's personal style. The other side of this 'fundamentalism' was however a lack of differential description. Today, especially in Europe, there is a noticeable change towards more specification and differentiation. Innovative work of that type has been done in different areas. One of the areas mentioned by Lietaer is working with the severely disturbed as practised by Prouty, and he refers to the chapter that Prouty wrote in his book, (Prouty, 1994).

Since we on the ward are building further on Prouty's work, we certainly identify ourselves as fitting this line of evolution as made explicit by Lietaer. Also his first statement sounds familiar to us, since we also made an evolution towards being more active in the therapeutic relationship. We also see ourselves as experts on the therapeutic processes of the people that are treated on our ward. As already mentioned we have an idea about what psychotic functioning is like, about how balances need to be restored and about the place, the importance and the method of working with psychosis and everyday reality in general. This will influence us in defining our priorities and subsequently organising the therapy we offer in a way that we think is most suited to our situation.

On the other hand, we don't want to make the mistake of having to choose sides in the discussion about what is more fundamental: the importance of 'being with' the client or the principle of 'doing something' with the client. This debate between a strictly non-directive, person-centred approach and a more process-directive, experiential approach is necessarily pragmatically overcome in our daily work. We would say that we regard the relationship as a crucial element and a basis to the success of more active interventions, as long as the client stays the touchstone of everything that is taking place.

Ward life
Essentially, we found out that restricting ourselves to only 'following or staying with the process' of a client in order to be therapeutic is not so easy when working in a residential setting. How do you meet this requirement concretely? How do you practise this 24 hours a day? What do you do when the things a client needs, or could use, are in conflict with the demands for management of

the other patients that are on the ward? What if, for example, somebody is lying on the floor and banging his head? This can be very meaningful and loaded with significance for that person at that given moment, but very conflicting with the house rules and the task of ensuring physical and psychological safety for the others present. What if the staff think that a certain person is mastering his psychosis enough so that he would benefit from an offer in the form of an anchoring exercise? Are we then still faithful to the Rogerian tradition of following the client's process?

To a lot of people, especially those who are person-centred and working in a ward setting, it is a continuous challenge to translate person-centred thinking to the treatment of a specific patient group, to this group of caregivers, in this specific setting, with its own structural demands, possibilities and limitations. The challenge is double: are our efforts 'person-centred' and are our efforts compatible with the demands of the setting?

In the next chapter, we will illustrate in detail how our therapeutic efforts are directly related to Garry Prouty's work and what our ward life looks like.

Chapter 2

A Contact Milieu

The ward

'Psychological contact' is the central organising concept for our psychiatric ward milieu. It serves the broad range of semi-acute to semi-chronic psychotic clients. 'Contact', which is seen as an antidote to psychotic alienation, from which all residents suffer, is the key word of the whole approach. The aim of such an approach is to restore and strengthen the ineffective Contact Functions so that basic contact with reality, affect, and communication becomes possible again. This all happens within a person-centred framework. There is a strong belief that we are working with human beings like you and me. We always try to separate the man or woman from the disease. Even if for the moment being, everything is rather chaotic or frozen, we continuously try to bring the person back into contact with, and in charge of, his own life. Frequently, progress first translates itself in an increased quality of life; a more 'being in contact' and more living in the 'here and now'. With the strengthened Contact Functions, people are better equipped to relate to someone who really wants to help them and to face their psychosis eventually. There is a conviction that we have to offer the patients the right conditions, so that it becomes possible again for the patient to use his or her own proactive forces, be it within the definite boundaries of vulnerability and scars from past history. We try to give back to the patients the mastery of their own lives. This is taken very broadly and is finally inspired by Rogers' notion of the fully functioning person.

In summary we try to guide the patients (and ourselves):

from a therapist–patient interaction that is characterised by interpreting, taking over, authoritarian, controlling, structuring, product-focused, judging;

from an activity that is characterised by being repetitive, superficial, empty, dull, obligatory;

from a level of functioning that is psychotic, inhibited, bizarre, isolated, non-accessible, insecure, covered-up, frozen;

towards a functioning that is experiential, process-oriented, anchored, in-touch, shared, decided, active, creative, varying, concentrated, enjoyed and in process.

Therapeutic organisation of the ward

Part of the treatment happens on the basis of *individual contacts*. The patient chooses one of the six psychiatrists of the hospital to follow them throughout their total stay. The psychiatrist is responsible for the (medical) treatment offered. Each psychiatrist is also responsible for one ward of the hospital. People with no preference are asked to take the psychiatrist responsible for the ward. At least once a week, there is an individual consultation to discuss progress and prescribe medication if necessary.

The ward has one psychologist (myself; 30 hours a week) who in principle works with every patient of the ward. If possible, this psychologist starts to work with someone even when still on the crisis-intervention ward, once it is clear that this person is a candidate for our ward. When transferred to the rehabilitation ward as a possible next phase in treatment, and when indicated, patients can continue seeing the same psychologist. If needed, a social worker is assigned. Nursing staff are available 24 hours a day, (i.e. 6.25 full-time-equivalent nurses from 7 a.m. till 9.30 p.m., and night nurses shared with another floor).

Part of the programme is offered to the whole patient group (20 'beds'). Evidently, living together and working with everything that this involves can be therapeutic. The nurses try to manage the ward with as much space as possible for the individual client. Each day of the working week we have a 10-minute meeting in the morning and in the evening, to open and close the day, presided over by the nurses. Once a week there is the ward meeting led by the psychologist with again everybody invited (see p. 90). Also the perception-training group is weekly (see p. 97). And at least once a month the nurses organise an outdoor leisure activity (see p. 95).

Occupational and movement therapy is done in subgroups. We call these routes. We have three groups each with its own target population and format:

Route I is meant for the more acute people, and people who have just arrived on the ward. Its aim is observation and preventing a further decrease in the level of functioning. The activities offered take place in a small group and are limited in time. There is a lot of attention given to a personalised approach.

Route II is indicated for people who want to build up their level of functioning. The activities take place in a larger group, take longer and demand more work, concentration and interaction.

Route III is for people whose first aim is to consolidate their regained balance. The activities are not too intensive but do take place in a group. There is a lot of attention paid to creating a pleasant climate and finding an appropriate pace for working.

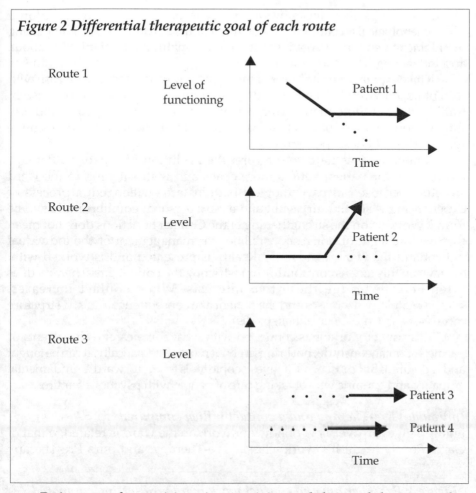

Figure 2 Differential therapeutic goal of each route

Patients can also participate in a creativity workshop and also in a number of activities that are open to everybody admitted to the hospital (swimming, day-workshop, aerobics etc.).

Basic to all this thinking about the translation of the contact paradigm into establishing a person-centred milieu is that we try not to deny psychosis, nor hide it, nor patronise the client. We see psychotic behaviour as pre-expressive behaviour. That means we see such behaviour as a way of expressing meanings that are there, but not yet fully in process or available to the person. Pre-Therapy helps to bring this message across, as a background inspiration and as a vehicle for concrete staff–patient interactions. Responding to a client from a Pre-Therapy framework can be built in systematically (e.g. in the organisation of the leisure activities or the weekly patient–staff meeting) or can happen very spontaneously. It can be aimed at either restoring absent contact, or at strengthening fragile contact. It is interesting to mention that these efforts can be done without neglecting the other tasks that we have to do. It also helps to make more appropriate observations from within a phenomenological attitude (meaning without immediate labelling, interpreting or judging patients and behaviour). It becomes a natural way of thinking about, and interacting with, the patients.

It takes some time and some training to become familiar and at ease with this philosophy, and this method of working. Even more so because in traditional education, many caregivers were trained to take action and 'do' things. Nobody ever told us that 'being with' the patient and giving simple reflections could be so powerful.

Sometimes it is hard to interpret the evolution of a patient. Perhaps temporarily the patient suffers more chaos and is threatening to the ward structure because old psychological patterns are challenged; a process of experiencing is starting up again and a new personal equilibrium has to be found. Working on the strengthening of the Contact Functions does not mean that we lose sight of our responsibilities for management of the individual patient and the ward as a whole. Reality is presented and is worked with, even when this means confronting or restricting the patient. Pre-Therapy does often help to bridge these two interests. When contact increases, symptomatology decreases and the patient as a consequence 'fits' the structure more (see e.g. *Crisis intervention*, p. 109).

This way of working is connected with what some caregivers, parents or partners spontaneously do, but brings it about more systematically. It can be taught and measured. But most of all, it gives people tools to put forward a fundamental empathic and genuine way of taking care of people with psychotic features.

Individual Pre-Therapy and a contact milieu compared

Figure 3 gives an overview of how our work on the ward is related to that of Garry Prouty. I call his work 'classic' Pre-Therapy, and ours Pre-Therapy

---

Figure 3: Pre-Therapy and contact work in a ward setting compared

	Classic P-T	Contact Milieu
Setting	individual	group environment
When	time-limited sessions	24 hours a day
How	formal sessions	spontaneous encounters/exercises
Where	office	ward
Caregiver	(psycho)therapist	contact facilitator
Clients' level	pre-expressive	'grey zone'
Therapeutic goal	contact restoration	contact strengthening
Therapeutic core activity	following client's process	bridging individual process and structural demands
Means	P-T reflections	contact work
Gateway	psychotic functioning	shared reality

translated to the organisation of a contact milieu. As you can see, distinctions can be made regarding setting, time, structure, the personality of the therapist, how and where sessions are organised, the level of functioning of the clients worked with, the therapeutic goal, the main therapeutic activity and the preferred gateway to reach and work with the client. (For concrete examples, we refer to the vignettes of concrete interactions p. 86).

Of course, this diagram is a simplification. It is drawn up to illustrate the differences in emphasis. Working in a ward setting naturally involves more unscheduled interactions. Nurses run into patients and work with them in their office, in the corridor, the living room and so on. They work with patients in the morning, during ward activities of all kinds, after visiting hours, on weekends, even at night.

We call the nurses contact facilitators rather than psychotherapists. They integrate Pre-Therapy reflecting in their daily work to re-establish contact and anchor the client. When the psychotherapeutic process becomes too intense or when formal sessions or interactions have to be scheduled, they refer to the psychologist (Pre-Therapy psychotherapist). When we say that they do 'contact work', we mean this in a broad sense. This includes of course using Pre-Therapy reflections indicated by a pre-expressive level of functioning. But most of the time, they are busy with strengthening the recovered Contact Functions. In an early phase of therapeutic evolution, very often people fall back to pre-expressive functioning, or pre-expressive and expressive behaviour are simultaneously present (see Figure 4). Working with this so-called 'grey-zone functioning' demands special skills. Therefore, the contact facilitator has to be guided by a correct assessment of the momentary level of functioning (see next section).

This all happens in occasional encounters (see) as well as through exercises and in the ward-activities that are especially designed to this end (see *Examples of spontaneous, informal use of Pre-Therapy Reflections*, p. 107). In all this, however, the 'shared' reality is also always encountered. Patients are by definition not only facing their personal therapeutic process but are also constantly and automatically confronted with, and invited to, anchor themselves in the reality we collectively live in — the ward setting, the reality of the here and now of the house rules, the physical limitations of one's body, the seasons, the visitors, finances, their room, the ward's lack of real privacy and so on. All these elements need to be consciously and constantly worked with and balanced.

Grey-zone functioning

When Garry Prouty describes his work, he mentions pre-expressive functioning as opposed to expressive, congruent functioning. In the latter case, contact with people, places, events and things (Reality Contact, RC), with emotional functioning (Affective Contact, AC) and other people (Communicative Contact) is given. In pre-expressive functioning, however, the restoration of these Contact Functions is the goal of Pre-Therapy. Matched with these levels, the therapist's methodology is well defined, respectively making Pre-Therapy

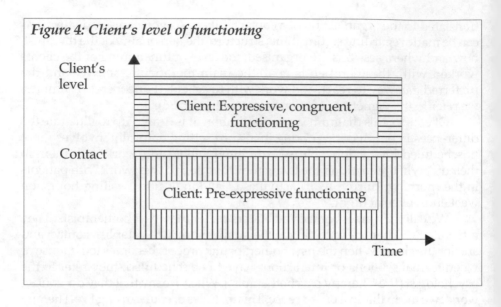

Figure 4: Client's level of functioning

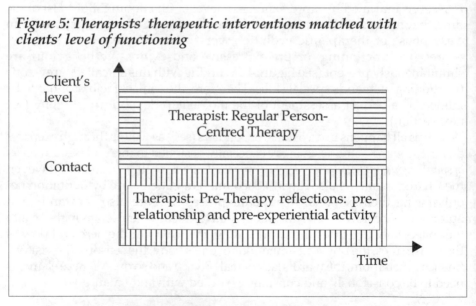

Figure 5: Therapists' therapeutic interventions matched with clients' level of functioning

reflections versus doing 'regular' person-centred therapy (see Figure 5).

In practice, however, the borderline between pre-expressive and expressive functioning is not always obvious. I call this 'grey-zone functioning'. In a certain area, the two modes of functioning are interwoven (see Figure 6).

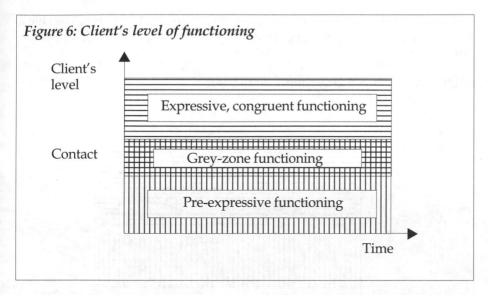

Figure 6: Client's level of functioning

Especially in our hospital practice, we often deal with people who function in that particular zone. Of course, therapist interventions have to be tuned in to this (see Figure 7).

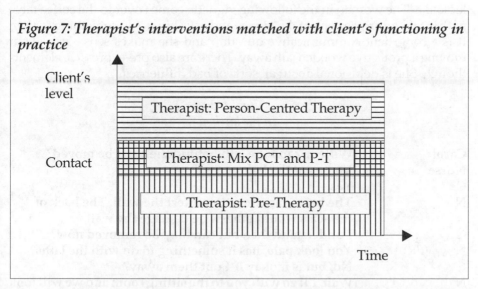

Figure 7: Therapist's interventions matched with client's functioning in practice

Our experience of grey-zone functioning clients helped us to specify our approach. So, besides the restoration of contact, the maintenance and strengthening of Contact Functions became the main therapeutic goals. We had to develop a good sense for estimating and working with the fluctuating level of functioning of the client. With our population, you need to master the Pre-Therapy reflections as well as 'regular' therapeutic interactions and be able to switch from one mode of working to the other if you want to be able to follow the client's augmenting/mounting/increasing or oscillating level of functioning.

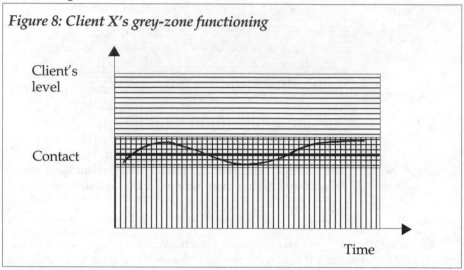

Figure 8: Client X's grey-zone functioning

I would like to give an illustration of what this grey-zone functioning can look like. The woman in the following vignette comes over to the coffee table of the staff, addresses one of the nurses and asks him to do something for her. It is a congruent communicative question and she makes sense: it is about moving a protective wooden lath away. There are also pre-expressive elements though. She is delusional about all sorts of bad influences.

Vignette
In the kitchen

Carol		**Willem, can't the lath behind the seats be moved?**
Nurse		**You want the lath moved?**
C		**Yes.**
N		**The beams are there to protect the wall. The back of the seats would otherwise damage the wall.**
C		**I understand that, but can they be removed now?**
N	(FR)	**You look pale, has it something to do with the laths?**
C		**No, but is it okay if I put them away?**
N		**Wait, I'll go with you to the sitting room and we will look at it together.**
C		**Only when you have the time, otherwise do not bother.**
		[Sitting Room, 2 minutes later]
N		**Show me!**
C		**Over there.**
		[Behind 3 seats, there is a lath on the floor, preventing the seats

from damaging the wall when they are placed flat against it.]
In my hometown on the market square, there is a timber trade and they do all different things over there and they are going to put me on trial and sentence me.
[Carol clearly starts showing her delusional world. The nurse shifts to Pre-Therapy reflections.]

N	(WWR)	**They are going to sentence you.**
C		**Yes, look, here's a lath, can't it be removed?**
N	(WWR)	**You would like the lath to be moved away and you are afraid**
	(RR)	**that they are going to sentence you.**
C		**Yes, because they are going to involve me in rituals of all kinds ... they are going to curse me, ... Can't these seats be placed over there? ... I moved those other seats around. Can't we do that over here with these also?**

[She is back on an expressive level. The nurse shifts up also and i.c. gives information and asks a question.]

N	**We** *[i.e. nursing staff]* **have put the same coloured seats together. Don't you like it?**
C	**No, it looks like a brothel.**
N	**I see what you mean ...**
C	**All right, I'm leaving you now. It's my job to do the dishes today.**
N	**Okay**
C	**Thank you, Willem.**

Since the client's anchorage in reality seems rather strong and since they are in the sitting-room of the ward with some other clients present, the contact facilitator chooses to stay close to her congruent messages and mix it with what we could call a reflective mode of listening. By that I mean that he uses Pre-Therapy reflections when a content is obviously pre-expressive. What is communicated here is that the nurse takes the client seriously. He doesn't cover up her delusional functioning or patronise her, nor does he choose the easy way of only hearing the congruent messages. They really want to understand each other. The psychotic pre-expressive element of her message drops when the conversation gets more and more concrete about the here and now, the perceivable and shared reality. She anchors herself further by setting aside her delusional thinking and fears and taking up her house keeping job of the ward again (strengthening reality contact).

The next case of grey-zone functioning illustrates how it was properly matched by the therapist's reactions. This is an interesting vignette because Reality, Communicative and Affective Contact became restored in one single interaction (See also Van Werde and Prouty, 1992; Van Werde, 1994).

Carol, age 25, has a history of admissions and re-admissions to general hospital psychiatric wards. Generally, her diagnosis was considered to be schizophrenic. During an acute paranoid phase, she is admitted to our hospital. She's continuously afraid that she will be murdered. Suicidal tendencies were observed. She is on neuroleptic medication. For the first two weeks she was under 'suicide-watch'. On a weekend, during a home visit, homicidal behaviour was manifest. She attempted to suffocate her younger brother to prevent him from being murdered together with her. She believes people she loves will be killed together, with her.

On the ward, this particular afternoon, the patients were discussing the hour at which they were permitted to leave the hospital for weekend visits. Officially, leave time is 2 p.m. People sometimes leave immediately after lunch at 1 p.m. To clarify these conflicting agreements, the staff decide that patients can leave that day at 1 p.m. with hospital permission. This vignette describes the concrete process between therapist and client about this issue of time.

Vignette

Nurse		*[I am sitting in the nurses' office. Carol walks in slowly. She sits down on the other side of the desk. She stares at me, her elbows on the desk. After a few seconds she asks a question, and simultaneously, quickly looks outside. From the corner of my eye I spot a bird flying away.]*
Carol		**Are they coming to get me?**
N		*[The hypothesis crosses my mind that 'coming to get me' has to do with looking outside and the bird flying away. If this is the case, then the patient functions at a pre-expressive level and Pre-Therapy/Contact Reflections are indicated. I choose to respond with Contact Reflections to keep that possibility open.]*
	(WWR)	**Are they coming to get me?**
N	(SR, RR)	**You look at me and ask if they're coming to get you.**
C		*[The client asks the same questions in the same penetrating way. This strengthens my hypothesis that Carol is in a psychotic state. The tempo of the interaction stays low.]*
N	(BR, RR)	**Just a second ago you looked up (I look at the window). You asked, 'are they coming to get me?'**
C		**I always hear aeroplanes and things.**
N		*[Carol shows something of her psychotic world. I accept this in silence. Eye contact remains.]*
	(WWR)	**I always hear aeroplanes and things.**
C		**What do you think? I want to know.**
N		*[It is not clear what she means with this question. Does she ask my opinion about the situation, about the interaction or about aeroplanes? Does she mean these things are going to take her away? I experience the blend of the two worlds: the reality of our conversation, and/or her paranoid psychotic system.]*
	(WWR)	**You ask me what I think.**

C	**Are they coming to get me?**
N	*[I feel every word is important. I don't know what she's going through or where these words are leading her. I'm careful and 'just' reflect what she gives. I make sure not to distract her or take her attention away from her process.]*
(WWR, RR, SR)	**Are they coming to get me? Just a while ago you said: 'I always hear aeroplanes and things'. Now you are looking at me and ask: 'Are they coming to get me?'**
C	**Can I phone home?**
N	*[This is a direct question. I give a congruent answer.]*
	No. We agreed on once a day and you already phoned home today.
	[This agreement was made during a family session. Carol used to alarm her parents unnecessarily several times a day by phone.]
C	**Are they coming to get me?**
N	*[Now things get even more complex. Probably her question is about her parents coming or not coming to pick her up at the hospital.]*
(WWR,SR,SR)	**You asked if they are coming to get you. You looked outside. I hear the sounds of engines, the sound of the motorway close by. I also hear music.**
	[I point towards the open window. Outside, probably someone is walking around with a portable radio. I stay with her process and bring in nothing new. With her words, I reflect the surrounding situation (noise and music). Next, I reflect her body. These elements all are possible points of anchoring.]
(BR)	**You shiver.**
C	**Can I phone home?**
N	**You already phoned. What did we agree?**
C	**They are coming at 2 p.m. It is still 1.30.**
N	*[This is obviously Reality Contact. How strongly she's anchored in her feelings remains hypothetical. I continue on a congruent level and make some suggestions.]*
	Indeed. So, what do you do? Perhaps walk around a bit. Perhaps you could lie down on your bed.
C	**Not on my bed, otherwise I think they will come and get me. I'm not sure I would survive.**
N	*[Probably through my suggesting, I induce her to become more psychotic again. So I return to word-for-word reflections and try not go beyond what she gives me.]*
(WWR)	**You don't know if you still would be alive then. You say: 'I'm not going to lay down, otherwise I think that they come to get me.'**
C	**I don't know if I will be alive.**
N	(SR, WWR) **You look at me and say: 'I don't know if I will be alive'.**

	(FR)	Your eyes look sad.
	(BR)	You shiver.

[Here, I have reflected not only her words, but also the larger surrounding reality: her body posture and her facial expression.]

C		I don't feel easy at all.
N		*[The client contacts her feelings: Affective Contact.]*
	(WWR)	You don't feel easy at all.
	(FR, BR)	You sigh, your head is in your hands.
	(SR)	You look at me.
C		If I go on a journey, it may be for the last time.
N	(WWR)	If you go on a journey, it may be for the last time.
C		I went to someone for advice and she said: 'You're going to make a trip and it will be your last one!' If I go, I'm afraid I'm not coming back anymore. Can I phone?
N	(SR)	I hear music in the corridor. Also, the cars on the motorway . . .
	(BR)	You stand up.
C		She can come and pick me up at 1 p.m.
N	(RR, WWR)	You stand up and say: 'She can come and pick me up at 1 p.m.'

[I think her level of reality functioning is up. I don't want to run the risk of frustrating her unnecessarily by not answering congruently. I think out loud about the confusing messages concerning the exact time of a weekend visit.]

Just a while ago patients were talking about the hour they could leave the hospital. Confusing probably!

[I take the phone.]

What's the number?

C		XXXXXX
N		*[The client very adequately gives the phone-number: Reality Contact. I pass the number to the operator and give the phone to Carol when the connection is established.]*
C		Is mother there? . . . Pass her to me . . . You can pick me up at 1 p.m. . . . the nurse.
N		*[This is very clear Communicative Contact with her mother!]* And?
C		When she finishes lunch, she'll come and get me.
N		*[The client starts crying and sobbing: Affective Contact.]*
	(FR)	So many tears!
C		Yes, and my mother says: 'Of course you can come and there will be other days too. It will not be the last time'. She wants to comfort me and says that nothing will happen. I wish I were home already.

N	(WWR)	**You wish you were at home.**
C		**I'll be glad when this is all over.**
N		*[She smiles: Affective Contact.]*
	(FR)	**You smile!** *[Carol leaves the office.]*

The patient opens the interaction with a question, so it's not clear what reality level she is operating from. The nurse chooses to give Contact Reflections. He doesn't fill in the meaning of 'come and get me' with reality. We see that, probably as a result, the client starts showing that there are at least two realities present in her question. First, there is the reality of the agreement made with her parents to pick her up at 2 p.m. Secondly, there is the reality of her paranoid fear of 'aeroplanes and things'. Also present is her paranoia about going on a trip, laying down on her bed, etc. This is obviously grey-zone functioning. In the course of the interaction, the realities that are mixed together and make each other unclear are separated. Psychological Contact (Reality, Affective and Communicative) is re-established and the confusion diminishes. The client anchors herself in the everyday reality and copes with it. She makes a phone call to her mother and changes the time agreement. She manages to go on weekend leave one hour earlier, is relieved and is even emotionally touched by her mother. The threat that something gruesome is going to happen disappears. The client improved her quality of living through the strengthening of her contact with reality, affect and through improved communication. If we recall that some weekends before, in a probably similar moment of grey-zone functioning, the client almost suffocated her little brother, we clearly see the value and relevance of anchoring and contact. An increase in someone's level of contact, no matter how small, can have great impact.

Whether or not you use Contact Reflections is determined by the continuous assessment of the client's level of contact functioning. This can be difficult, as illustrated in this case. When there is doubt, this therapist chooses Contact Reflections. These leave the most psychological space for the client. This problem of Contact Assessment in grey-zone functioning often occurs when a client asks a question. Is it congruent or psychotic functioning, or both at the same time?

When using Pre-Therapy reflections in grey-zone functioning, the client herself can 'decide' on which track she wants to continue. Or she turns back to (congruent communication about) the shared reality (as did the woman in the first example by taking up the dishes again) or the client decides to show more of her pre-expressive reality and starts processing it. This is what happened when the nurse in the second example said, 'You looked up and asked, "Are they coming to get me?"'. The client then revealed, 'I always hear aeroplanes and things', hereby showing and sharing another piece of her paranoid psychotic, pre-expressive world.

Also in the second vignette, after the congruent suggestion of the therapist to walk around a bit or to lie down on her bed, the client involuntarily falls back into her psychotic fear of people coming to get her, and her fear of surviving this. Later information raised the hypothesis of incest in that family. So the therapist's suggestion —although done in a sincere way— probably triggered memories and fears about lying down on her bed and waiting for somebody to 'come and get her'.

Notice how fragile this client is anchored and how powerful a remark that is made from outside her process can be. The fact is that you never know what something iatrogenic to someone's process can cause. Therefore, this therapist quickly gears back to Pre-Therapy reflecting, once he sees the destabilising and contact-impairing power of his remark.

Structural integration of contact work in the programme

As could be seen in the comparison of Pre-Therapy and contact-facilitating ward-work (Figure 3), rather than limiting ourselves to only giving reflections, contact work in its broad sense is the agenda of the day. This is accompanied by a paradigmatic shift. Instead of contact restoration, the strengthening of the Contact Functions is mostly worked on. This is because most people on our ward are already over the worst of their psychosis and are now struggling to consolidate the freshly regained anchorage. Besides, in individual encounters with the nurses or the psychologist (see *Examples of spontaneous, informal use of Pre-Therapy reflections*, p. 107) contact work is structurally integrated in several activities on the ward. As far as we know, this is unique. We give you an overview of how this is done in the weekly ward meeting, an interior decoration project, the organisation of leisure activities, the perception training group and other activities on the ward (as green work, starting several collections, and so on). This should illustrate in a very concrete way how penetrating the concept of 'contact work' is and how many possibilities there are to work along these lines.

The weekly ward meeting
In a lot of residential care, the available staff organise a weekly meeting with patients. It is rare that the framework and the goals of such an enterprise are clearly defined. Most of the time, such meetings are all about the lamps that need to be repaired or about the quality of the food... Such meetings get boring for staff and patients but are seen as a necessary evil. We try to make our goals explicit as well as trying to define what does and does not belong in such a meeting. We try to refine this element of our programme constantly. We feel it is a necessity to do so because in such a meeting the treatment philosophy is challenged and explicitly visible in how the staff chair the meeting and how they react to what happens and to what is reported about living together on the ward.

The ward meeting takes place each Friday from 10.30 till 11.15 a.m. With myself (the ward psychologist), the available nursing staff and all patients invited, we come together in the living room. It is a non-smoking event and one of the patients has as a job to open all the windows 5 minutes before the meeting to clear the air. The day before, during the briefing with the nurses, we go over the report of the previous meeting. We check if we followed up on certain points that were brought up and look for different subjects to talk about in the next meeting, for example, introducing a less cumbersome way to organise the meals at noon, announcing the arrival of new patients and so on. Attention is also given to how the group as a whole is functioning, which of the patients is having a difficult time and so on. If needed, the staff agrees upon who is going to do some contact work individually with a psychotic client before the meeting or who is going to sit next to him to work during the meeting if needed. Rarely, we decide that we need to ask somebody not to come if we consider that it would be too hard on him, on his fellow patients and on the staff. This does happen when somebody for example is too tired to stay awake, or is too psychotic so that he has practically no contact whatsoever.

The meeting starts with a short introduction about the goal and the rules. 'It is Friday morning, 11th of July, 10 hours 30. As each week, we come here together for our ward meeting till 11.15. It is an exercise to start a conversation and keep it going for 45 minutes. This is not easy, since we are all different. Some have difficulties talking, others talk to much . . . We want to talk about topics that can possibly be of interest to everybody. So these can be different things: the weather, therapies, the week that is coming to an end, next week, actualities, and so on. Things that are very intimate or private belong in a one-to-one conversation with the nurses, with yours truly or with your psychiatrist. So, which of you has a topic to talk about, a remark or a question . . . ?' If the staff have things to announce or to discuss, this is done at any moment in the meeting that looks best suited. The meeting has an open agenda except for two items: asking volunteers for the household tasks and, 5 or 10 minutes before the end, everybody is invited to say something about how they evaluate both the meeting and their contribution to the meeting. Wishing everybody a nice day and a nice weekend closes the meeting.

Immediately after the meeting the staff go over the meeting again. During this (15 to 30 minutes) evaluation, there is also space for personal feedback to the chairman or to other staff participants. A staff member then makes a report of the meeting, of the discussion afterwards and of the list of things to do or to follow up. This systematic way of working is not only beneficial for the meeting, but is also very educational for the nurses.

As an average, 15 to 17 patients out of 20 attend the meeting. We think that this success is due to the clear and explicit framework and goals that seem to be very relevant for this population. Also the appropriate balance between concreteness and abstraction and between open and fixed agenda items probably establishes enough security and trust for the patients to attend, especially since the whole enterprise happens in a welcoming and anchoring atmosphere.

In the following points, we will try to give you an idea of how this kind of meeting looks in practice.

On occasions it happens that somebody is overtly psychotic in the meeting; they may report bizarre feelings, or talk of idiosyncratic and highly private experiences without personal distance, or when formal disturbances of communication are present such as echolalia, word-salads and neologisms. Most of the time, this level of functioning can be dealt with by giving a few Contact Reflections. This often is sufficient to bring the client back into grey-zone functioning and have them participating again, whether it is by just listening or by simply being physically present without hindering the staff and fellow patients to proceed. Some examples of this application of Pre-Therapy in a group setting are given in another part of this chapter (see p. 112).

The meeting is structured around the need for the restoration and strengthening of contact. This contact-facilitating work is not a luxury given the fact that everybody on the ward has had a psychotic episode or is still suffering from it. We practise reality and communication, and also anchoring-work on the affective level is done but on a group level. This is a unique translation of Pre-Therapy thinking.

Strengthening communicative contact
As mentioned, at the beginning of the meeting we explicitly say that we consider this gathering as a communication exercise. It is not evident that one can sit together for 45 minutes with such a heterogeneous group of people if one doesn't value the fact of 'mere' talking. So topics such as the weather, traffic jams, music, how many eggs one is allowed to eat a week and so on, must not be regarded as trivial or as a burden. One has to realise that it is therapeutically valuable that someone can be attentive in a group setting for 45 minutes, and can practise this week after week. The participants don't easily talk spontaneously. If one wants to stimulate communication, one needs a lot of subjects to talk about with varying degrees of abstraction. Very concrete topics probably appeal more to people who are still very much locked in their world. More abstract themes, a discussion or information are probably more suited for people who function on a higher level.

Meeting for 30 minutes turned out to be too short, as one sometimes needs more time to talk about some emerging topics, whereas 60 minutes turned out to be too long for the average patient — the level of fear of the unstructured got too high. The meeting is not a task force, nor a mere skills training group nor a psychotherapy group. It is a mixture of all this since besides being task-oriented there is always space to talk about anything, be it emotional or interactional. Group dynamics come into play and can get rather heavy sometimes, when deciding who is to preside over the meeting, and this has to be taken into account.

It is best to be lead by the group as to which topics interest them most at that time. We once had a Scottish historian visiting us, so you would think that there would be enough talking points. It turned out that only starting from the very concrete here and now of the Scottish checked skirt of one of the patients could get a conversation going. Other themes were psychologically probably too distant or remote.

Another thing we learned is that there is only conversation as long as something actually has happened on the ward, if people participated or at least felt involved in ward life and everything that went on. People with psychotic features rarely talk social talk and certainly not in a group. Emptiness — their own as well as that of wardlife — can be highly present. We discovered that subjects in which particular patients or staff members have a special interest do very well. It becomes possible to talk about the closing down of the Flemish coalmines if someone from the region of Limburg — a former coal area — talks about how he lost his job. Or there can be talk about old trades when people know that one of the staff members weaves baskets in his spare time, and a German visitor from Heidelberg was personally addressed by one of the patients who used to be a professional printer and knew that Heidelberg was a brand name of world famous printing presses.

Mostly, somebody from the staff introduces a theme that connects with ward life, actuality or the group at that moment. Short interactions emerge around the different themes. Some patients talk, others follow more or less actively, others are absorbed in their private world but stay present, others need to leave the meeting for some minutes (to go to the toilet, because they are too stressed, an irresistible need to move etc.) and come back in. The chairman makes sure that everything that is said is audible and paraphrases, reflects and invites members to enter the conversation. Sometimes a theme comes up about which there seems to be a lot to tell, and spontaneously there is a conversation that associatively shifts from one aspect to the other. A conversation about the telephone started by someone's remark that the national phone company was promoting their own brand of fax copier. The conversation then went to 'green numbers' (free calling), wireless devices, videophones, a new phone in the lobby of the hospital and a changing of phone numbers in our area. In such moments, we need to closely watch time and stop the conversation if we want to have some time left to distribute the housekeeping jobs and do the evaluation at the end. I prefer to chair the meeting together with one of the nurses who organised that week's leisure activity. She can bring in a lot of reality and by doing so stimulate communication. It is an advantage if someone from the staff who has to work the following weekend is present too. The meeting gives, in 45 minutes, a lot of information about what is going on on the ward, how the relationships between patients are and the psychological state of every individual.

Reality-oriented work

During each meeting a lot of attention is paid to offering themes from, and talking about, everyday reality. For example we mention at the start of each session, that there still is a lot of cigarette-smoke in the room, that somebody new is expected on the ward, that there is construction-work going on nearby causing traffic jams and delay for visitors and so on. Sometimes we use a playful way to offer and strengthen contact with reality. We might ask of what herbs the bunch on the table is composed; how long the sun is up today (e.g. at the beginning of the summer, the longest day of the year was so may hours, minutes and seconds, as shown by the detailed information on the day-by-day calendar); how heavy the pumpkin is that Group II grew in the garden and so on. Regularly, we also bring information from 'outside' inside. Something from the newspaper ('a man-made vehicle on Mars'), from the radio ('the Gulf war just started') or from someone who just arrived ('glazed frost on the road').

Often the house rules are repeated or freshened up as a follow-up of something that recently went wrong or in connection to a certain atmosphere: 'Nobody is allowed in someone else's room', 'No nightwear in the living room'. Sometimes points that are brought up are referred to where they belong with an explanation why. Someone's request to reduce medication, for example, belongs in an individual contact with his/her psychiatrist. Information about 'medication' in general can be given or discussed in the group. In such a way, people get a better hold of the structure, on the how and the why and on their place in the whole system.

We also do a lot about anchorage in time. We try to keep the tension between the previous, the current and the next meeting. Sometimes somebody is quoted from a previous meeting ('You proposed to rent a movie, Jos'), or we continue on points from the last meeting ('You said that you would call the museum to know the opening hours and the rate for groups, Goedele'). The support of contact with reality and time can become very concrete. We have a noticeboard on which we pin all the information that we have on a scheduled trip (leaflets, newspaper articles); we have a folder were we keep all the used and acquired information on trips, visits and so on; we keep a hand-written cookbook with all the dishes we prepared on the ward etc. Of course all this has an informative value but it also helps to make people more aware of time and of their personal history ('Next week, I'll be visiting this', 'Three weeks ago I participated in the baking of an apple cake'…). For confused people this often means a rare moment of solidity; for more chronic people these events are the only things that bring life and variation in their monotonous world. Being occupied with all these themes supports a lot of patients' elementary sense of reality and gives opportunities to anchor themselves in it further.

Working on affective contact
Coming together regularly enhances the possibilities of seeing what goes on on an individual and on the ward level. Remarkably rarely is something said about it spontaneously. We hypothesise that a lot of people who suffer psychotic functioning during and around the meeting do not know that they also experience some reality-based and proper affects. By actively picking up themes with an emotional undertone and by presenting this in the group, people can check within themselves if they recognise something, identify it and give it a name. This in itself is therapeutic. Feelings are contacted and spoken about. A step is made, people get more in contact with themselves, some (emotional) tension goes out of the air and that brings some relief.

There are a lot of themes that are cyclic and have an affective load like saying goodbye, being admitted in a hospital, being on medication, just to give some. Themes like 'emptiness', 'dependence', 'passivity' are always indirectly present in the meeting but are hard to get on the table. This would probably be too confronting and would frighten people away.

If a certain topic is addressed, we always bear reality- and affective-communications in mind. If a particular topic comes up we have to be aware that as well as the obvious meaning it contains it can also trigger emotional meanings for others as well as for the person himself. The latter rarely emerge spontaneously, but if they do, they are very unexpected. So someone can perhaps run into his fear of emptiness by a conversation about organising a TV-free evening on the ward, or someone can discover her anxiety about being alone with her husband when hearing somebody announce his discharge from the hospital and going home happily. Often one only notices that emotionally a lot must have happened during the past week, after systematically reviewing it. So once in one week, two new nurses started on the ward, and several students were participating in labour and movement therapy in connection with a mental health project. In the ward meeting, we reminded the patients of all these realities and made space for what this has meant emotionally. We asked who remembered that all this happened last week or we said that we ourselves found it a busy week with a lot of new faces and offered the hypothesis that maybe this has meant a lot to some patients too.

When we as staff members go over the meeting afterwards, we sometimes discover that we missed some points that were probably playing an important role in the affective life of some of the patients: once we forgot to mention impending Fathers' Day. Sometimes we go over to the next topic too early or we realise only afterwards that as an answer to someone's question we too easily generalised and gave information without making space for affective elements that without doubt were present in the question. For example, somebody asked about the absence of a nurse and we replied that indeed she was on leave to have a baby without asking if somebody had something to say about that, or without asking if there were any mothers among the patients or similar inviting questions.

So, during the meeting, we limit ourselves to actively making space for naming emotions without going in to them in detail and without processing them. It is not always easy to draw a clear line between these two forms of working with feelings. So we do not do psychotherapy as such in these meetings, but we do restore and strengthen affective contact. This is a direct translation of Pre-Therapy thinking, as is working with the threatened Contact Functions which is a leading thread running through the meetings.

Leisure activities

Another example of how we try to counter unnecessary alienation by constantly and structurally offering the possibility for anchorage, is the way we organise the ward's leisure activities. These activities consist of visiting a museum, playing games, taking a walk, etc. We gradually became aware of the contact-enabling possibilities of these activities. For instance, near the village where our hospital has its grounds, the University of the city of Gent has tropical glass houses in its botanical garden. We used to go there, but don't do so any more because this milieu isn't the kind of place that anchors our patients. They already have so much difficulty staying in touch with the 'normal' surrounding reality that we don't wish to confront them with an artificial, tropical environment with strange exotic vegetation, high temperatures and a high degree of moisture that is very unusual, not to say unknown in our climate. Nowadays we go regularly to a woman two blocks away from the hospital who has a very pleasant herbal garden and cultivates bees and honey. She shows us around her garden and shares with us her expertise on nature. By doing this, we are working with what is growing here and now and this sharpens contact with everyday reality. It also opens up people to all kinds of processes including cyclical processes that are visible in nature. We return regularly so that not only our knowledge of botany, but also our personal relationship with the woman, her garden and her pets, can grow. She sometimes comes over to our hospital to walk in our gardens and to talk about 'our' plant life. These are experiences that we value very much because they are so anchoring and foster a phenomenological attitude.

Since we work with a group of twenty patients, from the acutely psychotic to those recovering, we always have to design a contact opportunity that appeals to people on whatever level they are functioning. People who are in a more acute state only need a very concrete activity whereas others need more. They maybe drawn to reproduce some artwork that we have seen or to prepare a speech on a topic that they are especially interested in or have expertise about. We have to be aware of different levels of anchoring and start from there. We don't want to appear exotic or extreme, but on the other hand we don't want to get trapped in nationalism. We have had people on our ward from other cultures and we offered them the chance to anchor themselves back in their native culture too. We had, for example, a patient whose second language was English. She was Belgian but was raised in England. When she was staying on our ward — and responding to a request from several patients — we got her to give some lessons in basic English language to her fellow patients and nurses. For her, that was anchoring since she could relive a part of herself that had been hidden for so many years. For other people in our programme who were sufficiently anchored, is was a challenge to try out their notions of English. Another patient, with grandparents in India, led a cooking activity. She made a rice dish with specific herbs that she brought along. For the woman herself, it meant anchoring her back in her native culture since she was born and lived for some years in India. For some interested others, it was enriching to meet her as a person and through her to meet another culture.

We try to make sure that we don't overdo it, so we organise only one leisure activity a week. If we go out, we try not to combine this activity with other things. If visiting the museum in itself takes a lot of energy, we use our own transportation to get there and avoid complicated bus changes and so on. We try not to overload the programme because the people who need anchoring most are the people who function at the lowest level.

Interior decoration
(with thanks to Joseph Van Akoleyen)
As another illustration of how thinking in terms of contact strengthening penetrates daily life on the ward, we highlight an interior-decoration project that was set up to help people become aware of their cultural identity again. We thought that also cultural anchorage would be a constitutive element of psychological well-being (see *Levels of anchorage* p. 116) and by definition the opposite to psychotic alienation.

We decided to place different culturally anchoring objects in the living rooms (see also Van Werde and Van Akoleyen, 1994). We had, for example, jars with shells from the Belgian North Sea beach − Belgium has a coast and most people go there for the holidays and come across shells and sometimes collect them. We also had jars with Belgian stamps. We had some replicas of Belgian monuments like the Lion of Waterloo − a landmark to remember the defeat of Napoleon in Belgium − and the 'Atomium', the Belgian pavilion of the World Exhibition that took place in Brussels in 1958. We had an old map of Belgium on the wall with every small village mentioned. In this way everybody had the chance to reconnect with the village or town where they were born or once lived. We had original Belgian comic books of the Smurfs, Lucky Luke, Kuifje (Tintin) and so on. We had books about famous Belgian people like Eddy Merckx, the cyclist, and Father Damian, who worked with lepers in Molokai and who was declared blessed by Pope John-Paul II in Brussels recently. We had a piece of famous Belgian lacework framed on the wall. We saw that these objects did what they were supposed to do, that is they offered a way to contact a larger (cultural) identity. People − patients as well as staff members and visitors − said things like, 'Oh yeah, when I was a child we visited the Lion of Waterloo with our class', or 'My grandmother lives near the sea and she has a collection of shells that is similar to the one here', or 'I used to own a lot of comic books before I got ill'. So the project stirred up individuals by confronting them with culturally relevant things. There was a great deal of communication, much identification took place, and considerable contact was facilitated. In people who were not so verbal, we could see faces change when they came into contact with one of these objects. We could reflect their facial expressions and start from there, working towards affective contact through responding to, and connecting with, such low-level and yet very concrete aspects of their being.

Perception-training group
(with thanks to Chris Deleu)
In the observation-training group, the participants learn how to connect with reality again. They become more than passive observers of the world. Usually

people restrict themselves to a mere fraction of what is offered to their senses and mind. In phenomenological observations, however, there is a participating awareness, based on openness oriented towards the world.

Training exercises are offered once a week in a 90-minute group session and they are aimed in the first place at awakening or arousing the capacity for observing in a healthy manner. It is not only hearing and seeing that are addressed, but also, and especially, those senses we need to be aware of our own bodily or personal physical space (Soesman, 1987). In so-called negative symptoms and also in the side effects of neuroleptic medication, we see how poorly anchored psychotic people are in their bodies and in the larger reality. Strengthening this anchorage is done through different kinds of exercises (tactile, motor, balancing, auditory and visual).

Approximately half the patients in the ward regularly participate. The group is open and heterogeneous: those who have experienced their first psychotic episode and are recovering, chronic sufferers, incipient psychotic persons. Some have only recently been admitted; others have been in the hospital for months. This brings a complexity which demands a highly personalised approach, a basic phenomenological attitude and more than a little common sense. The exercises take place in different locations, even within a single session: the therapy room, in the garden or the wood of the hospital, in a natural resort nearby and so on. Different kinds of resources are used: sticks, little bags filled with rice, drawing material, musical instruments, minerals, reproductions of artwork, participants' own bodies, plants, clay, sand and a Cretan labyrinth 26 metres in diameter. Exercises can be accomplished alone, in twos, in small groups or in the whole group. Short intensive concentration exercises can be done, but also a walk lasting a whole afternoon is scheduled every season. The theme also varies, but it is always connected to the rhythm of the year (seasons, Christian holidays and so on). During each session, people are free to drop out and to watch for a while if they feel like it, for not everybody is capable of actively participating for the whole 90 minutes.

It is significant how intertwined the Pre-Therapy and observation training-group approaches can become as they are implemented in our residential therapeutic programme. We find them complementary in the sense that both work with observations: the first focuses on strictly private and psychotic observations and the latter on 'realistic' ones. Pre-Therapy helps to re-establish contact with reality, emotions and other people, whereas observation-training structurally supports and strengthens these Contact Functions and by doing so builds up the possibilities for further healthy functioning. Both prove essential if we are to address psychotic experiencing in a therapeutically fruitful manner.

Various group activities

During the years that we have worked on the ward, we have seen a lot of projects emerge that can be seen as influenced by Pre-Therapy thinking. As mentioned earlier when talking about the ward meeting (see p. 90), and also in the projects, it became obvious that something can only take form if there is somebody from the staff who is really enthusiastic about it and is willing 'to pull the cart'. It needs a lot of motivation and personal investment to make something happen. Often discussed by the nursing staff is their disappointment about patients doing so little by and for themselves. Sometimes even feelings of revenge or retribution can be spotted among staff in utterances like, 'Why should we bother, if they don't seem to mind?', 'Why do we always have to organise activities for them, why don't they take more responsibility for their own lives', 'When they don't come up with topics to talk about, we won't speak either!' As mentioned earlier, working on a ward for psychotic people means frequently being confronted by passivity, energy loss and psychological 'emptiness'. To prevent burn-out, one needs to find a healthy balance for oneself when — even indirectly — challenging these major topics.

Green work
What is more anchoring than following nature in the changing seasons of the year? We try to be attentive to that, integrate it in the daily ward life and explicitly talk about it in the ward meetings ('the leaves are turning brown'; 'now, wild strawberries can be found in the meadow'; 'mushrooms are popping up in the wood', 'did you notice that there are new-born lambs etc.'). We very consciously work with all this and theoretically label it as restoring and strengthening contact with reality. Talking about it is seen as strengthening communicative contact. This is rather easy, since nature is a relatively neutral and commonly known subject to talk about. When emotions arise, they are mostly feelings of surprise, wonder and curiosity. This affective contact is enriching for somebody's life, rather than threatening freshly recovered balances. These experiences also foster a phenomenological attitude, i.e. they learn to use a welcoming, non-interpretative attitude themselves, which proved itself very valuable in their therapeutic process. Many activities can be based around natural material: in spring, we cut off a branch, put it in a vase and watch how it buds; we plant a tuber, keep it in the dark and go check it every week to see how it is growing; we plant a small herbal garden with all herbs in it that can be used for drinking tea on the ward (sage, lemon balm, camomile and mint); we use vegetation for Christmas, and Easter decorations and so on.

Collections
As a way of cultural anchoring (see *Levels of anchorage* p. 116), we try to stay in touch with what's going on in everyday society. It helps people to stay connected with life outside the institution. We for instance started several collections that a lot of people have nowadays. We collect things like trading stamps, used telephone cards with different illustrations on them, 'flippos' (little plastic collectable discs that are enclosed in products like potato chips), and so on. With these things, we started ward collections. Everyone is invited to contribute if he or she is interested, however small his or her contribution may be, and invest in a large collection. The good thing about it is that this is a

playful, innocent and non-threatening way of doing something together. Also, these collections are constantly 'in process' and growing. It also underscores the importance of working together to achieve a common goal — on a meta-level all very encouraging and stimulating messages. Regularly talking about the collections, exchanging items, making overviews of what we already have and are still missing, fosters a lot of genuine interaction since something is really happening on our ward and consequently, there is really something in common to talk about.

'Reality' lessons
We offer people some group meetings about certain topics. For example we had 90-minute sessions about how to take the train, how to use a telephone book, personal grooming and so on. We consider this as working on strengthening contact with reality. Of course, similar activities can be organised in other therapeutic settings too, but we also find them perfectly compatible with our philosophy. Even the person-centred framework is not violated since no one is forced to take part. Everyone is invited. For people whose Contact Functions are restored, but who are not certain enough about how to proceed on certain occasions, these lessons are very welcome and matched to their individual process. This is what we meant when stating that we are person-centred and active or 'process-directive'.

Contact-facilitating work in occupational therapy
(with thanks to Luc Mulkers and Etienne De Buck)
I would like to illustrate how in the multi-disciplinary approach, and more specifically in occupational therapy, a significant translation was made of Prouty's Pre-Therapy. It became integrated in the occupational therapist's everyday way of interacting with the patients. This is a result of a process of getting familiar with Pre-Therapy and having had supervision-sessions about possibilities and difficulties in applying this new input.

Instead of, or besides being, product-focused in doing occupational therapy with people who are low- or out-of-contact, a more process-oriented way of interacting with this kind of patient took shape. As the practice of 'reflective listening' illustrates, working in this sense not only has the effect of establishing contact with the patient, but is also strongly motivational and helps to bring the patient in contact with the material to work with. Psychotic experiencing is left for more congruent interaction with the other (the therapist) and the world (the material). Sometimes, troublesome affective functioning can be put aside if contacted and listened to in an appropriate person-centred way. When dealing with our kind of clientele, this process often involves using Pre-Therapy reflections. One occupational therapist reports: 'Besides offering the more traditional activities, bit by bit, a ward-specific way of working with these psychotic patients was developed. I understood that contact is a premise, as well, if one wants to work together, just as one would work with material, in a meaningful way. When making acquaintances, in a first session, during therapy or when socialising with the patients, I consciously and unconsciously started to use more reflecting.'

The experiential world of the client became the point of view to connect with and start from. This resulted in a more existential contact between therapist and patient, and the patients more personally engaging in activities. In general, more space was created for independence and taking responsibility for their own activities. People were enabled to choose to be active and do things, or not. Acceptance of, and an ability to make contact with, their lived world was the keystone of this shift. There used to be an accent on performance and result, but it shifted to being with, and doing things together. After being listened to in a Pre-Therapy mode, people now often can – even temporarily – put aside their psychotic experiencing and concentrate on their world. This increases the level of their Contact Functions. This building up of strength is beneficial to perhaps addressing psychotic experiences later, without running the risk that their everyday healthy functioning gets constantly totally overthrown.

Also the therapist himself felt more connected/engaged when working along these lines. He states: 'Events, actions, verbal and non-verbal acts used to be neglected, corrected or interpret by me rather quickly. But now, out of a genuine interest for, and belief in, the healing power of making space for low-level experiencing, I think I give more real chances to the patients. I experience this personal evolution as an enrichment of my therapeutic abilities. The clients also seem to like this new style and seem to benefit from the improved contact with themselves, with their environment, with each other and – of course – with the material.'

Examples of this particular way of interacting with the patients can be given:

(SR)	**I see a lot of smiling faces in your collage.**
	You are using a yellow pencil.
	Willy is here also.
	You tear up your drawing and throw it in the waste bin.
(FR)	**You look sad.**
	Your eyes are wet.
(BR)	**You are rocking.**
	You make a fist . . .
(WWR)	**You say that it is very hard for you to sit here.**
	Yes, Mr. Devil.
	Bah . . .
(RR)	**Yesterday you told me that you heard disturbing voices.**
	Last week you drew a face, now you're drawing a face.

When doing this, psychological space often becomes available again, and contact with therapist and the material arises as a natural outcome of not being absorbed in a private autistic world anymore.

As a general remark, we can also state that behaviour that earlier would be classified as 'not appropriate', 'not adapted', 'psychotic', 'non-functional' and thus contra-indicated for participating in occupational therapy, now is considered as a connecting point or a stepping stone for real contact, the beginning of an interaction that could result in functioning on a higher level and make full participation in occupational therapy possible.

Often, these interventions can hardly be called Pre-Therapy; I prefer the term 'reflective listening'. It is important that as a caregiver you have the existential and theoretical depth to validate pre-expressive behaviour. Then, given the setting and the level of the people you work with, it can be beneficial that you integrate the reflections in your way of working. In other words, this means that you are capable of adjusting your own level to the level of the client, that you learn to pick somebody up at a lower level and jointly shift to a higher level of functioning. In grey-zone functioning, this way of working can look a little bit ridiculous when you see it on paper. That is because you don't fully sense the presence of low-level functioning. Very often also, this level is covered up by seemingly congruent functioning (like asking a question, doing organised things, etc.). It is a pitfall then to — by definition — proceed only on these apparently congruent elements. This is what patients know so well: this is how they keep hidden their real hurt, their confusion and their personal story. I think that you at least should give the message, and be able to offer the possibility, that together these doors can be opened some day. Of course, all this is only possible if the client can trust, if he wants to and if he is ready for it.

It is often rather easy to shift somebody up to the congruent level by reacting only to the congruent part of his functioning. This can be a very appropriate decision in a ward or non-verbal therapy situation (labour therapy, movement therapy, perception-training exercises). On the other hand, you would be surprised at the depth of your contact and interaction if you would manage to stand still at the other (low-level) elements that are often there under the surface too. As we said in the case-illustration of the grey-zone functioning (see p. 81), the reflection of 'Are they coming to get me?' made it possible for the patient to disclose a paranoid psychotic world whereas immediately interpreting the patient's question as a fully congruent message would have paid no respect to these hidden elements, to this lived reality. What makes it worth trying is that you not only support or restore the endangered Contact Functions, but that you bring the person back in contact with his own psychological power, his own resources so that he can make his own decisions again, and stop his surrounding from making the choices.

Some small vignettes now follow, of people who function on a grey-zone level and who are approached by Pre-Therapy listening. The patients are not fully concentrated on their work since their private experiences are to disturbing and demanding or too much in the foreground. Pre-Therapy reflections are used to connect with the patient to clear some space and to consequently bring him more in the here and now.

Bart

Bart interrupts his activity and starts staring outside. The therapist reflects this to bridge this episode of possible contact-loss and prevent further drifting away towards psychotic functioning.

Therapist	(SR)	**You look outside . . .**
Bart		*[No visible reaction.]*
T	(SR, RR)	**You turn/twist/play with your pencil and you look outside . . .**
B		*[Starts drawing again.]*
T	(SR, FR)	**You draw again . . . And you look up . . .**
	(SR)	**You look at me.**
B		**. . .**
T	(RR)	**You look at me, just a while ago you looked outside.**
B		**I want a cigarette.**
		I'm staying so long on the ward already . . .
T		**So long already . . .**
B		**Next time, I'll make something in clay, as a farewell gift for my psychiatrist . . .**
		[Starts laughing in a bizarre way.]
T	(FR)	**You laugh . . .**
	(FR)	**I see tears in your eyes . . .**
B		**What will I be doing at home all day long . . . ?**

Then, the therapist also shifts to a congruent level and they talk about the patient's fear of leaving the hospital and not being able to master his free time. They discuss day care as a possible bridge between full-time and no admission. After this, the patient was able to put aside his worries and started drawing again, without being distracted by his thoughts and fears for the near future anymore.

Harry

Harry is a young man, 23 years old, with a chaotic contact. Since he functions on a low level, he is oriented towards Route I (the small group with an intensive and individual approach — see p. 78). His motivation, co-operation and emotional moods fluctuate continuously. His lack of concentration, attention and endurance, make him very difficult to work with or to have him function in a group setting. He likes to have all the attention and his behaviour if often immature.

That day, Harry arrives late and without his keyboard for his daily musical lesson of fifteen minutes. He comes in and puts his head on the piano.

Therapist		Hello Harry.
		[H. stays with his head on the piano.]
T		Hello H.
		[H. says something unintelligible, stays with his head on the piano.]
	(SR)	You said something . . . I couldn't understand . . .
	(SR)	Your head is on the piano . . .
		[H. stays a little while in the same posture. Suddenly he starts to cry.]
	(FR)	You're crying . . .
		[H. is continuously crying and stays in the same posture.]
	(RR, SR)	You're crying with your head on the piano . . .
		[H. lifts his head . . . sighs . . . dries his tears from his face.]
	(SR)	You're looking at me . . .
	(FR)	You sigh . . .
	(FR)	I see tears on your face . . .
	(SR)	You dry away your tears . . .
H		Synthesiser . . .
		[H. is silent, lets his head and shoulders down.]
T	(WWR)	Synthesiser . . .
	(RR)	Last week you were here every day at the same time with your synthesiser . . .
	(BR)	You let your head and shoulders down . . .
H		I don't feel like playing today . . . I'm too tired . . .
		[H. looks into the eyes of the therapist and starts shaking his hands.]
T	(SR)	You're looking at me . . .
	(BR)	You're shaking your hands . . .
H		I didn't practice this weekend.
T	(WWR)	Didn't practise . . .
H		I had a quarrel with my father.
		[H. lets down his head, looks sad.]
T	(WWR)	You said you had a quarrel with your father . . .
		[H. keeps silent.]
	(BR)	You let your head hang down . . .
		[H. remains silent, no reaction at first sight.]
	(FR)	You're looking sad . . .
H		My father is so severe, each evening I must go to sleep at 9.30, even in weekends . . .

From that moment, Harry starts talking fluently and on a congruent level about himself and the things he's occupied with: the disturbed relationship between father and son and the communication problems they have. In a 'normal' conversation, they talk briefly about these things. In this way, the right mood was created to proceed with the activity planned for the session. As a first step, contact was established; then interaction and activity became possible.

It is worth noting the difference between 'expression' and 'contact'. I always find it a way of neglecting psychotic people when they are left in their psychotic functioning without help. If somebody constantly reverts to his psychotic experiencing, I consider this as mere expression, without the person being in control or without the possibility of deliberately choosing this activity. When you work from a Pre-Therapy framework, the importance is stressed of being with what happens, of at least offering the possibility to (re)connect with the shared reality, with the patient's own affective sources – where all the 'crazy' functioning comes from – and connect with the human beings that surround them and want to help. In a way, this is what happened in next interaction.

Mary

Mary is a middle-aged woman. Just like last week, she enters the therapy room with her typewriter, right on time. She doesn't speak, looks extremely tense, starts working even without any reaction to the therapist and his welcome. She starts typing something without structure, without goal, mechanically. In our line of thought, you could compare this with mere 'expression', in the sense of quasi-involuntary or mere repetitive actions comparable to a car driving by itself without someone at the steering wheel.

Therapist(SR)		**You're typing . . .**
		[M. keeps on typing. Suddenly she looks up.]
	(SR)	**You're typing . . .**
	(BR)	**You look up . . .**
		[M. looks down, sits at the back of her chair and goes on with typing.]
	(SR)	**You look down . . .**
	(SR)	**You sit at the back of your chair . . .**
		[M. makes eye-contact.]
	(SR)	**You look at me . . .**
		[M. stops typing.]
Mary		**Do they build a home for old people?**
T	(WWR)	**Do they build a home for old people . . . ?**
M		**I hope they build a home.**
		[M. is silent for a while and than starts typing again.]
T	(SR)	**You are typing . . .**
	(WWR)	**You hope they build a home.**
		. . .
		. . .
	(FR)	**You look sad . . .**
	(RR)	**You hope they build a home . . .**
M		**In Gent!**

T	(WWR)	In Gent . . .
M		I don't feel well . . . I can't work today.
T	(WWR)	You don't feel well . . .
	(WWR)	You can't work . . .
	(RR)	You hope that they build a home . . .
M		My mother . . .
T	(WWR)	Your mother . . .
M		She's getting older and she's not doing well.
T	(WWR, RR)	She's not doing well . . .
		You're hoping they build a home . . .

From then on, there was a certain contact, based on the feelings and thoughts that kept her busy in the moment, more specifically the question of whether her mother could be sent to a home for elderly people nearby the place she lives. After an open and realistic conversation, Mary was ready to do some 'real' typing since contact was made and the things that had occupied and distracted her were listened to and could be put aside. They agreed that she would copy a text on certain herbs that grow in our garden that the nurses of the ward had been asking for.

Movement therapy and contact work
(with thanks to Paul Gistelinck)

In movement therapy, Pre-Therapy reflections are used to mirror empathically the position in space and the expression of the patient at a certain moment. This is done to strengthen the Contact Functions by confronting the patient with his 'body-ness' and to make him aware of his body as being expressive.

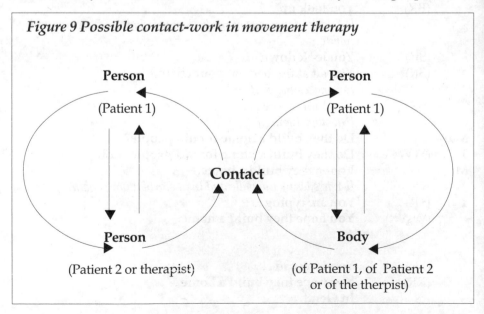

Figure 9 Possible contact-work in movement therapy

Person
(Patient 1)

Person
(Patient 1)

Contact

Person
(Patient 2 or therapist)

Body
(of Patient 1, of Patient 2 or of the therpist)

Illustration
After an intense session, the therapist offers relaxation. One of the patients doesn't lift his left leg, as instructed. The therapist reflects, 'Your left leg is on the floor' (BR). The patient contacts reality again and replies: 'Oh yes, I was dreaming away'. Possible drifting away in a highly private and psychotic reality was prevented and the patient was able to join the session again, which was also therapeutic.

Examples of spontaneous, informal use of Pre-Therapy reflections
(with thanks to the ward's nurses)

Short interactions
1. The wife of a patient learned to use facial reflections whenever her husband was at home and 'drifting away' as she called it. On the point that he was just beginning to lose contact, the use of reflections could prevent him being drawn into pre-expressive functioning. In my opinion, relatives can be trained for applications like this. We did not do it systematically yet, since the power of the reflections should not be underestimated as they can be very intensive and aggressive if not used in a proper way! In the above mentioned case, the woman was a speech-therapist and occupational therapist, thus used to giving reflections and used to matching the tempo and to taking into account the psychological state of the client. Also to her advantage was that she was a relative, knew her husband very well and could easily recognise the facial clues correlated with the start of a psychotic episode.

2. In the book *Nausea* by J. P. Sartre (1988), we find an example of how a man applies what we can call Pre-Therapy reflections to himself, in order to avoid further panic. In casu: the person uses situational reflections to strengthen his fragile reality-contact with the objects in the street.

> An absolute panic took hold of me. I no longer knew where I was going. I ran along the docks, I turned into the deserted streets of the Beauvoisis district: the houses watched my flight with their mournful eyes. I kept saying tot myself in anguish: Where shall I go? ANYTHING can happen. Every now and then, with my heart pounding wildly, I would suddenly swing round: what was happening behind my back? Perhaps it would start behind me, and when I suddenly turned round it would be too late As long as I could fix objects nothing would happen: I looked at as many as I could, pavements, houses, gas lamps; my eyes went rapidly from one to the other to catch them out and stop them in the middle of their metamorphosis. They didn't look any too natural, but I told myself insistently: This is a gas-lamp, that is a drinking fountain, and I tried to reduce them to their everyday appearance by the power of my gaze. (pp. 114–15)

I have come across several people who spontaneously applied things like Pre-Therapy reflections, without being familiar with Prouty's work. The teaching and application of Pre-Therapy reflections as a kind of anchoring skill for family, patients or ex-patients is another field that could be explored.

3. It is 2.15 p.m. The nurses are in a meeting at their office. Paula knocks on the door and enters. Her knees are bent, her face looks like she is in pain and she says that she's suffering vaginal bleeding. Earlier, with the same complaint, another nurse had checked her condition and had not found any bleeding. One nurse reports: 'I go with her to her room. Paula sits down on her bed and leaves no room for me. So, I take a chair and sit down opposite to her. She sighs'.

Nurse (FR)	You sigh, Paula.
Paula	Yes, of course! Wouldn't you? All that bleeding! What's going on?
N (WWR)	Bleeding, you say ...
P	Yes! *[She smiles.]*
N (FR)	You smile ...
P	It is nothing to laugh about, you know!
N	*[Partially reacting congruently and partly with a FR.]* No, I see that your eyes look sad ...
P	*[She is silent for a while.]* Yes, and my mother was going to call me at 1 p.m. and she still didn't call!!
N (FR, WWR)	Your eyes look sad ... You expected a phone-call from your mother at 1 p.m. and she didn't call yet.
P	I have to go to the bathroom now. Will you return at 3 p.m.?
N	*[Answering on the same congruent level ...]* Yes, I'll be here at 3 p.m.

Paula enters with an obviously pre-expressive, psychotic message. The nurse listens to her and tries to bring her back in contact with what she is trying to express with the help of Pre-Therapy reflections. As a result, the patient shows that it is hard for her to wait for something that her mother promised to do, but didn't do yet. Paula does contact her feelings of impatience, communicates them and as a consequence, becomes more able to cope with the reality of the situation. This short informal interaction was sufficient to bring the woman back in contact with herself. The crisis did not escalate and she became able to express what really was on her mind. Probably the waiting-for-her-mother has been very hard and had been psychotically translated.

The nurse provided the right climate. By her own strength, the patient could again congruently express what was going on. The nurse took her seriously and met her on the same level of concreteness. The patient consequently made the next step and disclosed what was really going on: she felt upset since her mother had kept her unexpectedly waiting.

4. Another nurse reports: 'The patient had just arrived on our ward. She was behaving very agitatedly, like she was on speed (talking a lot, singing, slamming doors, pacing, radio at maximum volume, yelling in the corridor…). Suddenly, she pulls open the door of our office and yells: "I'm going to listen to music now! OK? Good? I'm going to do it now! See you!" I responded: "I'll walk with you to your room"'.

Pauline	**What is this all about?**
Nurse	*[I give a congruent answer and say . . .]*
	I just want to talk to you.
(FR)	**You look surprised …**
	[We enter the room and sit down on her bed. She starts to laugh.]
(FR)	**You laugh aloud …**
	[I notice that on the contrary, her eyes look sad.]
(FR)	**You look sad …**
P	*[Patient embraces me and starts crying.]*
	Maybe my sister is happy, but I'm not. She's not unhappy, I am.
	[Then she keeps silent for some seconds, stand up, says that she is feeling better and that she is going out for a walk.]

Good observation of the face and the use of facial reflections were helpful in bringing this patient back in contact with what was really going on in her mind. It also helped to slow down her tempo and it made some psychological space for more constructive action (relating to the nurse and going out for a walk).

Crisis intervention
This illustration comes from an interaction that took place on the locked crisis-intervention ward of our hospital. The nurse who witnessed the event reports: 'When Barbara was admitted, it was very difficult to get in contact with her. It was like talking to a brick wall: nothing seemed to get through. The psychiatrist decided that she should have an injection of neuroleptic and sedative medication since she was overtly psychotic, had a poor sense of reality, was agitated and had no insight into her way of functioning.'

That afternoon, two nurses are struggling with Barbara to give her the injection. She is fighting and screams very loud. When hearing all this noise, I come running to the ward to see if my help is needed (as is the silent agreement between that ward — situated on the floor above my office — and myself whenever there is something going wrong). I enter and see a difficult situation. The patient is very agitated and screams things like, 'I know everything. Let go of me. I am not crazy.' The nurses are considering the patient's transfer to the ward's isolation-room and tying her to the bed. With the help of myself and a third nurse that came running to help, the injection is given. The patient stays agitated and screaming. The nurses try to give her some psychological space to find out if she wouldn't calm down by herself. This doesn't work. She paces up and down the room, looks like a cornered animal that wants to run away and repeatedly yells out her partly paranoid-psychotic, partly comprehensible messages. There is a lot of medical equipment in the room and I fear that she will start throwing bottles and other stuff around soon.

My estimation is that this woman will not calm down by herself. When she is asked a question, she does not manage to give an answer but continues to scream and to repeat the same sentences. It seems that she does not take into account the disturbance she makes. On the other hand, I strongly have the impression that this woman wants 'to get rid of something', like there is a certain message hidden in her overtly spoken words that she wants to transmit. She over and over repeats the same things, but nobody really seems to pay attention, and listen to it. The nurses repeatedly try to reassure her that everything will be OK, that they will release her when she has calmed down, that they don't think that she is crazy and so on, but she doesn't listen to them either. She is also constantly given the opportunity to give an explanation, being asked what she means by 'I know everything', but she does not manage to say anything that seems directly relevant to making herself better understood or enabling the nurses to take care of her in a more effective way.

Meanwhile, the real fighting is over, there is still tension in the air and everybody is taking deep breaths to recover from the intense physical (inter) action. I take advantage of this moment by trying to make contact by means of Pre-Therapy reflections. I hypothesise that contact is needed; the woman is extremely psychologically isolated. Everybody wants her to do things, which she obviously isn't capable of doing yet. Probably she feels herself totally misunderstood and even violated. The things she wants to communicate are condensed in a few sentences that are too cryptic to comprehend and about which she can't give further explanation. At the same time, though, I sense her power. She wants to communicate something and fights to make herself understood.

She wants to be heard. Maybe this has to happen first, before she will submit herself to the structural demands of the ward situation (being quiet, taking medication, proper communication, staying inside, etc.).

I stand besides her, breathe along at her tempo (BR), make eye contact and empathetically say, 'You take deep breaths' (BR).

Barbara   *[Sighing, taking deep breaths.]*
Dion (FR, BR)   **Pfft . . .**
                     [A reflection inspired by my own breathing out.]

B		*[Starts pacing again, stands still and stares . . .]*
D	(FR)	**You look like you're thinking...**
B		**I know everything!**
D	(WWR)	**I know everything!**
	(RR)	**Just a moment ago you screamed, 'I want to go home' and 'I'm not crazy'!** *[and on a higher level]* **There is a chair, if you want to sit down . . .**
B		**. . .**
		[No visible nor audible response.]
Nurse		**The zipper of your skirt is still open.**
		[The zipper had been opened to give the injection.]
B		*[Pulls the zipper to close it. It is obviously stuck but she pulls again, doesn't want help, and tears the lining . . .]*
		I know everything.
		[So partly in contact with the reality of the zipper but partly still dwelling in her pre-expressive psychotic world.]
D		*[I have no idea what she is talking about. Is it a congruent message or paranoid or both? I choose Pre-Therapy-reflections and want to enable her to choose whether or not she wants to communicate congruently or stay in her psychotic world . . .]*
	(WWR)	**I know everything.**
	(RR)	**You were screaming . . . you yelled very loud . . . 'I know everything!'**
B		**I only did not see my children!**
D	(WWR, RR)	*[Also this message is unclear to me. But I very strongly sense the meaningfulness for her and also her attempt — albeit rather indirect or difficult to understand — to bring across something that is of quasi-vital importance to her. I also notice that she no longer repeats one of her standard sentences and that apparently something is changing and seems to process . . . So I very much try to be with her message and carefully reflect her words).*
		I only didn't see my children.
		[I repeat this sentence a few times because I see that this is very contactful B and myself now almost constantly have eye contact, and B definitely becomes quieter. I strongly have the impression that I really enter her world that in one way or the other I reach her. She maybe even feels understood. Her concern and intensity had come across to an other human being — even without the other exactly knowing what it was all about.]
D		**Look, if you want to, you can sit down on this chair.**
		[In an attempt to take care of her further. Patient does not react to my remark. She goes to the window and stares outside.]
D	(FR)	**. . . as if you're thinking . . .**
B		**I want to make a telephone call.**
		[Now B is definitely calmer. The one remaining nurse takes her

> *to a phone in the corridor. B asks the operator for a line but no*
> *connection is established; probably B gave a wrong number.*
> *Nevertheless, B seems satisfied. The nurse and myself escort her*
> *to her bed. She lies down, eyes closed and looks very tired.]*

This problematic situation was countered through the use of Pre-Therapy reflections. By the power of the encounter of two persons, by the empathic understanding that came across, the patient no longer resisted. Without Pre-Therapy force probably would have been necessary to prevent worsening of the situation. I would say that the degree of disorganisation was inversely correlated with the degree of contact.

Different kinds of Pre-Therapy reflections were used in this crisis-intervention situation. Remarkably, the therapeutic effect was obtained, even with the caregiver not understanding the content of the message. The overall effect of the intervention was that the patient got more affective hold of herself. Also her contact with reality increased, as did her communicative ability (asking for a line to the operator, giving a number — even an incorrect one). At first she was obviously stuck in pre-expressive functioning; later on she congruently formulated a question. The therapist opened himself to the whole person, thus looking further than only the behavioural aspects. Sometimes it can be required to cut through the situation and take over control (for example, by taking the patient to a separate room). Pre-Therapy taught me, however, that somebody is often capable of more than was thought possible at first sight if you are able to offer the Rogerian conditions and if you are used to work with such ways of (pre-) experiencing and (pre-) relationship by means of Pre-Therapy reflections.

Additionally, this intervention strikingly illustrates that being non-directive (meaning non-authoritarian, non-manipulative, non-steering) and using Pre-Therapy does not necessarily contradict the structural demands of the setting. No glass bottles were thrown around, nobody had to be isolated in a separation room and the patient did calm down.

The use of Pre-Therapy reflections within a group setting
As we described earlier within the therapeutic organisation of the ward, some activities or therapies are scheduled for subgroups and some happen with the total ward population invited. We discovered that even in such moments, Pre-Therapy reflections can be used.

Pre-Therapy in its pure form is always indicated to work with low-level-functioning people. Most of the time when in a group setting, it is the caregiver that is hesitating to use reflections. Maybe they doubt their own skill, feel uneasy, silly or childish, or maybe there is not enough privacy with other patients present.

In our experience members of the group understand very well that by giving reflections, the facilitator is trying to be helpful by establishing contact. This is a very positive message. It means that the caregiver indirectly expresses his trust in the proactive forces of the patient, that he tries to build up the strength of the person he works with. It also means that a psychotic episode doesn't automatically leads to repressive interaction but instead is dealt with in a very accepting and containing way.

Of course, before the start of certain activities as for example the weekly ward meeting — as described on p. 90 — the staff each time discuss if someone is being prevented from participating this time since his or her overall functioning is considered not to be manageable. The following can be called examples of sudden and momentary psychotic functioning. If patients are too psychotic, they wouldn't choose to attend a group event anyhow. On the other hand, when functioning on a grey-zone level (see p. 81), participating in a group event can be so stressful that a fall-back to clearly pre-expressive functioning can be triggered. However, we are always welcoming and respectful of the effort of somebody to be present, even without verbally participating. As you will see in the illustrations, using Pre-Therapy reflections can augment somebody's level of functioning just enough to enable them to stay present. The fellow patients who witness this kind of interactions most of the time feel relieved that he or she is 'with us' again and that psychosis didn't take over. This is a struggle they all feel connected with, since this is the common base on which they are all admitted and treated on this particular ward.

Illustrations
1. During the ward meeting, Chantal suddenly stands up, points at the window and says, 'I see them moving again'. I reflect word for word and also the anxious expression of her face. This intervention seems to anchor her. She looks around, becomes aware of the group again, sits down and the meeting can proceed.

2. Willy arrives ten minutes late at the ward meeting. He is carrying a Bible, walks straight up to me, takes no notice of his fellow patients sitting in a circle, points to words in the text and says: 'I can make the letters change'. I make eye contact, point to the text also (BR) and reflect: 'Willy, the group is meeting (SR), you are standing up (BR)… next to me (SR) . . . You show me the Bible (SR) and say, "I can change the characters" (WWR).' As a consequence, Willy reconnects with the reality of the meeting. He takes a chair and quietly sits down at the outer side of the circle.

3. In an other ward meeting, Thea — an adolescent mildly mentally retarded girl — is continuously wobbling on her chair, obviously not at ease and occupied exclusively with her private world. Sometimes she giggles and says shreds of sentences that don't fit the context. Her fellow patients give her a lot of credit even though she can be very disturbing sometimes. We try to keep her in the meeting by regularly reflecting what she does or says: 'Sometimes, you stand up for a while. You giggle. We were talking about the ward's coming leisure activity and you say, "At school, pfft . . . Yes, than they found me and took me to their home I suppose…"'

Our impression was that this girl needed this kind of continuous support to enable her relatively to master her ongoing pre-expressive functioning. She couldn't manage it by herself and it even looked like she made the group meeting less frightening by speaking her thoughts out loud and treating the others as audience rather than as interlocutors. In individual sessions, she would stay practically mute and show less of her psychological process than in the group meetings.

4. With everybody entering the living room and the staff ready to start up the weekly ward meeting, Carol, a patient, comes hurrying in and continuously babbles. Obviously she is very upset. It is the same patient as on p. 84 who was then also delusional about a wooden object.

C   **In the cafeteria there is a crucifix in bent wood! There are seances there! I am permeated by smoke and I do smoke more lately!!**

T   (WWR, FR) **Carol, you just were in the cafeteria and you saw the crucifix.**
You look upset.
You talk about seances and smoke.

C   **Yes, the closer you get, the more you smoke!**

T   (FR, RR) **You look concerned. You just came running in from the cafeteria and you obviously go through a lot now . . .**
[By giving the reflections, the patient's pre-expressive functioning was received. She found someone to share her turmoil with. This enabled her to put her concerns in the background and direct her attention to the group meeting. Her delusional thinking came back when we at the end of the meeting – like we always do – asked everybody to say something about how the meeting went. When it was her turn, she said . . .]

C   **I don't know what it is ? The smoke of the cafeteria is already in here also!**
[Then – referring to the rules of the game – the chairman/president/ psychologist asked her to focus on how she evaluated this meeting. Carol was able to say that she had been busy with her thoughts mainly and that following what was said by the others had been too difficult for her.]

Chapter 3

Afterthoughts

Therapeutic process

By constantly paying attention to the contact level of the client, we discovered how complex therapeutic progress can be. Distinctions can be made between the level of contact with reality, contact with affect and contact with others. In a psychotherapeutic process, these three Contact Functions probably don't have an identical evolution.

In Figure 10, we see that in the beginning Reality Contact, (RC), Affective Contact, (AC) and Communicative Contact, (CC) are situated on a obviously pre-expressive level (P). The evolution of the different Contact Functions reaches a grey-zone level (i.e. sometimes pre-expressive, sometimes more on a congruent level). RC moves fastest and crosses the contact threshold first (Q), and is first to clearly reach a congruent level (Q'). Communicative contact follows the same pattern but later in time (RR'). Affective contact on the contrary stays pre-expressive all the way.

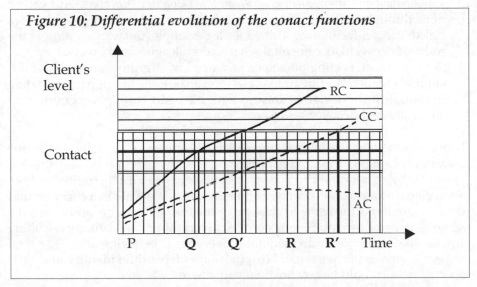

Figure 10: Differential evolution of the conact functions

As seen in studies carried out by Prouty (1994, p. 45) often Reality and Communicative Contact respond earliest and most to Pre-Therapy reflecting. The augmentation of Affective Contact is probably harder to establish. This should not surprise us, since Prouty's research is often carried out on people functioning at a very low level with presumably very stressed affective functioning. What is important for us at this point is the idea that maybe Reality, Affective and Communicative Contact can be separately influenced. The relevance of these thoughts is significant; more so if we think of ward settings were there are a lot of ways to, for example, focus on and work with reality and communication. It implies that the route to exercises, product-oriented and scheduled activities is now open. The bridge is made between following individual process and working with the given reality within the borders of a specific setting and without losing the person-centred attitude.

Levels of anchorage

Theoretically, we can speak about different layers of anchorage that go hand in hand with different kinds of remedial contact efforts. We talk about four different types and these can serve as reference points in deciding the kind of contact we wish to offer to the clients with whom we work.

1. *Existential contact.* The right simply to exist and to be recognised as a member of humanity. This right is supposedly guaranteed by society.
2. *Psychological contact.* The concrete awareness of reality (people, places, events and things), of affective states and the ability to communicate all this in a congruent and socially understandable way. When absent, individual Pre-Therapy can be used to restore this kind of contact.
3. *Consolidation and strengthening of the restored Contact Functions.* This can be done through individual exercises or together with other people in a so-called 'contact-facilitating' milieu as, for example, the ward-setting of the residential psychiatric hospital where my colleagues and I work.
4. *Cultural contact.* Feeling ourselves part of a larger group can (re)build our cultural identity. We illustrated how this can be done through participating in thoughtfully designed leisure activities and through encountering culturally anchoring objects (see p. 95 and p. 97).

In our ward setting, we deliberately work on these ideas. Gradually we became aware of how subtly this kind of anchoring plays its part in every day life. For example, being admitted to a hospital can serve as an illustration of how alienating a move to another environment can be. We walk in a corridor, and the corridor looks the same as the one of the hospital nearby, and much the same as in any hospital in your country. Everything looks alike, everything smells alike, everyone is dressed alike, everyone is behaving alike. The total impact is sterile, not personal. Hospitals often have little identity and little specificity — it could be any hospital, anywhere.

A number of questions and two answers

Let me start to say something about what it takes to work along Pre-Therapy lines. People often ask me if it is not too time-consuming and thus cost-inefficient to integrate this reflective contact-facilitating style. Will the daily routine of the nurses, for example, be thrown aside in favour of only, and strictly, psychotherapeutic interactions? Will there have to be separate rooms to do Pre-Therapy in? Will the house keeping still been taken care of when everyone is engaged in non-directive therapy? Is it wise and meaningful to go along with madness or incomprehensible things? Isn't medication the only thing that really can help people who function on such a low level? Isn't Pre-Therapy a risk for the safety of the personnel . . . what about aggression, body contact . . . ? Aren't you over-emphasising psychosis?

I have two answers to this. Workers in the field easily recognise Pre-Therapy as something that a lot of them were already (more or less) doing. The different kinds of reflections don't look so strange to them, especially when the personnel have experiences with small children. Children ask that they be related to in a concrete, low-level way. That is what you need to do if you really want to reach them.

The '70–30' idea
When building a contact-facilitating environment, the tasks that existed before still have to be taken care of after introducing Pre-Therapy. In a ward setting, patients need to get their meals, pills and attention. Their rooms need to be checked, leisure activities have to be scheduled, group meetings take place, people must be reminded to the therapy hours, they need support, their family must be listened to, the weekend leave has to be prepared and so on. I call this the 70% of the work that basically remains the same, whatever approach you follow, whatever therapeutical song you sing. We could estimate the latter as specific, be it only 30% of the whole work.

But the 30% makes the difference. In our situation, this means that staff personnel need to be trained in Pre-Therapy and schooled in contact-facilitating thinking. This smaller portion of the work will influence also on the 70%! It is like a little bit of leaven that defines the taste of the whole bread. This is to say that:
- the new inspiration can easily be integrated
- it does not alter the everyday activities so much
- it still can have an enormous, determining impact on the essence and outlook of the care that is given.

Part 2 References

Deleu, C. and Van Werde, D. (1998) The relevance of a phenomenological attitude when working with psychotic people. In: B. Thorne, D. Mearns and E. Lambers (Eds.) *Person-centred Therapy: a European perspective.* London: Sage.

Gendlin, E. (1968) The experiential response. In: E. Hammer (Ed.) *Use of Interpretation in Treatment.* New York: Grune and Stratton, pp. 208–27.

Lietaer, G., Rombauts J. and Van Balen R. (Eds) (1990) *Client-Centered and Experiential Psychotherapy in the Nineties.* Leuven: University Press.

Prouty, G. (1994) *Theoretical Evolutions in Person-centred/Experiential Therapy: Applications to schizophrenic and retarded psychoses.* New York: Praeger.

Rogers, C. (1966) Client-centered therapy. In: S. Arieti (Ed.) *American Handbook of Psychiatry.* New York: Basic Books, pp. 183–200.

Sartre, J. P. (1988) *Nausea.* Harmondsworth: Penguin Books, p. 114–15.

Soesman, A. (1987) *De twaalf zintuigen.* Zeist: Vrij Geestesleven.

Van Werde, D. (1994) 'Werken aan contact' als leidmotief van de wekelijkse afdelingsvergadering in residentiële psychosenzorg, *Tijdschrift voor Psychiatrie, 36* (8), 46–53.

Van Werde, D. (1995) Contact-faciliterend werk op een afdeling psychosenzorg. Een vertaling van Prouty's Pre-Therapie. In: G. Lietaer and M. Van Kalmthout, *Praktijkboek Gesprekstherapie.* Utrecht: De Tijdstroom, pp. 178–87.

Van Werde, D. (1998) 'Anchorage' as a core concept in working with psychotic people. In: B. Thorne, D. Mearns and E. Lambers (Eds.) *Person-Centred Therapy: a European perspective.* London: Sage.

Van Werde D. and Prouty G. (1992) Het herstellen van het psychologisch contact bij een schizofrene jonge vrouw: een toepassing van Prouty's Pre-Therapie, *Tijdschrift Klinische Psychologie, 22* (4), 269–80.

Van Werde, D. and Van Akoleyen J. (1994) 'Verankering' als kernidee van residentiële psychosenzorg. *Tijdschrift Klinische Psychologie, 24,* (4), 293–302.

Van Werde, D. and Willemaers, R. (1992) Werken aan contact: een illustratie van Pre-Therapie met een chronisch psychotische vrouw. Seminarie en Laboratoium voor psychologische begeleiding, Rijksuniversiteit Gent. Video tape with brochure.

Further reading

Gendlin, E. T. (1970) A theory of personality change. In: J. Hart and T.M. Tomlinson. *New Directions in Client-Centered Therapy.* Boston: Houghton Mifflin, pp. 129–73.

Merleau-Ponty, M. (1964) *L'Oeil et l'Esprit.* Paris: Gallimard.

Peters, H. (1992) *Psychotherapie bij Geestelijk Gehandicapten.* Amsterdam/Lisse: Swets and Zeitlinger.

Thorne, B. (1992) *Carl Rogers.* London: Sage.

Van Dam, J. (1981) *Fenomenologie en Therapie.* Oegstgeest: Bolkbericht 2.

Part 3

Marlis Pörtner

Pre-Therapy in Europe

Chapter 1

The Pre-Therapy Project at Sint-Amandus

Introduction

The *Psychiatrisch-Centrum Sint-Amandus* in Beernem near Bruges, Belgium, was founded in 1928 by the Congregatie van de 'Broeders van Liefde'. Since then, numerous 'architectural' and conceptual changes and innovations have taken place. Today the centre sees itself as a modern psychiatric clinic focused on the individual and offering a wide range of therapeutic approaches. The hospital contains wards for acute and chronic patients as well as for people with mental difficulties, a nursing home, day and night care units and sheltered apartments. Originally conceived for men only, since 1990 the hospital admits women too. However, men are still considerably in the majority, especially in the chronic wards where there are practically no women. Sint-Amandus has room for 745 patients, 519 at the clinic itself and 226 at the connected nursing home (where gradually 116 beds are being removed), there is a staff of 593 (sharing 490 established posts).

Since 1989 there has been a Pre-Therapy project for chronic patients. In December 1996 I was offered a week-long opportunity to get to know this programme at first-hand. I followed the staff members at their work and extensively discussed the various aspects of the project and their experiences of it. I was deeply impressed and learned a lot during this week. On the one hand I could see, once more, what long-term hospitalisation does to a person and how, despite many positive innovations in psychiatry — and this is true not only for Beernem — some traditional structures and attitudes, especially in the chronic wards, are tenaciously persisting. On the other hand I could watch committed professionals doing their best to change these attitudes, taking the patients seriously and responding to them. And I also witnessed how, even with completely secluded and so-called 'hopeless' patients, sometimes suddenly the 'little flame' (as Dion Van Werde once called it) appeared and for a moment the person, buried under disease and decline, was visible.

The history of the Pre-Therapy project

'We had a very unsatisfactory situation,' explains *Dr Luc Roelens*[1], psychiatrist at Sint-Amandus and founder of the programme. 'There were too many patients we could not reach by psychotherapy.' Together with some co-workers they began to consider this problem thoroughly, studying literature and looking for new ways. Through Gendlin, who came to Leuven in 1983, they heard for the first time about Garry Prouty. They started to read and discuss Prouty's papers without, at first, knowing too much about what to do with it.

The crucial impulse came in 1985 with Prouty's workshop in Breda. Now Luc Roelens recognised the relevance of this approach showing new ways of working with chronic psychiatric patients. Above all he was convinced that it was a practicable approach, not tied to Prouty's charisma (though his charisma is undeniable). It was concrete, observable and comprehensible and could be used by other people and transferred to their own work situation. After the workshop, Luc Roelens wrote a paper where he summarised his impressions and considerations, with the intention of making this new therapeutic approach known at the hospital. He hoped that the clinic would immediately recognise its importance and support its introduction. Yet, not until 1989 did the time come when Luc Roelens could start the programme and invite Garry Prouty for a seminar at Sint-Amandus. In between, the psychologist Bea Coninckx had got to know Prouty's approach too by participating in the second workshop he gave in Breda in 1987.

At Sint-Amandus several preliminary events were organised in order to prepare the participants thoroughly for Prouty's seminar at the clinic. It was very important for Luc Roelens to establish a concrete connection with the staff's everyday work at the hospital. Psychologist *Paul Lambrechts* and occupational therapist *Geert Gruyaert* prepared roleplays where the nurses performed those patients they had particular difficulties with. Bea Coninckx and Luc Roelens gave lectures on the theoretical foundations of Pre-Therapy. Dion Van Werde too was invited to give a lecture. During the seminar itself, the prepared roleplays were played together with Prouty who took the roles of the nurses. Thus, with the help of their own work situation, he could give the staff hints about how to respond to their patients in a Pre-Therapeutic way.

Originally the programme was intended primarily for the nurses. The founders felt that the nurses had the most opportunities to apply and integrate Pre-Therapy into their daily work. Luc Roelens had not anticipated the solid resistance from the staff that came to oppose his idea. In most wards, there were two or three people interested in Pre-Therapy and willing to try it. But they felt quite isolated because the majority of the nurses could not see any

[1] Names have been italicised on their first appearance in the text, at the author's request, as a modest sign of appreciation and gratiude for their commitment to Pre-Therapy, and for allowing the author to use their experiences and material in this publication.

good in this approach and resisted it. Sitting with a patient and trying to make contact, in the eyes of many nurses, was not 'real work' and not anything serious. Instead they felt it was their duty to 'do something'. On the wards where this attitude predominated, it was deadening for those who actually were motivated to try Pre-Therapy.

However, for some members of the staff, meeting Garry Prouty turned out to be a key experience that fundamentally transformed their way of working and their attitude towards the patients. They refer to times 'before Prouty' and 'after Prouty' and emphasise how much more satisfying their work became 'after Prouty'. These staff members are the ones who, together with *Bea Coninckx* and her team, often under very difficult conditions, to this day keep Prouty's approach alive at the hospital and contribute to its further evolution.

In 1978, an occupational therapy project group had been founded with Bea Coninckx and several occupational therapists, among them *Leo Dumon, Chris Van Wyngene* and *Els Coghe,* with the aim of developing better therapeutic ways of dealing with chronic patients. At that time this was primarily seen as a matter of stimulating the patients' activities. The initiatives were always started by the staff in the hope that the patients would join in. The work of this project group was based on humanistic psychology and its phenomenological foundations and started from the hypothesis that activities would lead to contact. However, it turned out that only about 80% of the participants could be reached, and this only in a very superficial way. They participated mostly in indifferent, impersonal and somehow mechanical ways. The assumption, that activities would lead to contact, was not confirmed.

In 1989, Prouty's seminar at Sint-Amandus showed the four therapists new perspectives for their project. Prouty provided the theoretical foundation and a practical concept, specifically designed to stimulate and foster experiencing and contact functions of these chronic patients. Based on the principles of Client-Centred Psychotherapy and on their own experience, they carefully began to work with Prouty's contact reflections. They formed a 'Prouty-group' with 21 so-called 'not accessible' patients. In the group sessions, which were held twice a week, the therapists individually responded to each patient. The emphasis now was on developing contact functions, and the infrastructure was shaped in order to facilitate and encourage contact. The therapists were no longer trying to activate the patients; they just wanted to be with them and focused their attention on each person's contact initiatives.

After a time of getting to know each other, significant changes could be observed with the patients. Particularly even with the most contact-impaired people a relationship had developed, whereas with others short verbal exchanges became possible. Others, after some time, even felt solid enough in their contact to be able to express fragments of their inner world and of their experiencing and began carefully, together with the therapists, exploring and processing them.

It was not a smooth shift as at that time the project group still was part of the occupational therapy group. It was difficult, in terms of staff and structure, to establish equally optimal conditions for both, the new project and traditional occupational therapy. Fortunately Dr Roelens had the overall responsibility for the project. Due to his position as a psychiatrist he was able to back up the team who could always count on his support. Another psychiatrist, *Dr Hugo Huygens,* had been fully behind the project from the very beginning, and all the other psychiatrists of the hospital were at least positive. This considerably helped to overcome the initial difficulties.

Since 1990, there are regular interdisciplinary Pre-Therapy meetings, chaired by Luc Roelens. The founder and his co-workers meet with those of the staff who are actively interested in Pre-Therapy: Bea Coninckx and the occupational therapists working with her, including a movement therapist, a speech and language therapist and all the nurses who are interested in and wanting to work with Pre-Therapy.

1994 Prouty gave another seminar at Sint-Amandus, the main topic of which was how to deal with hallucinations. The same year, the Pre-Therapy project, under the name PGCB (persoonsgerichte contactbenadering), became autonomous and further consolidated.

The PCCB project

Today Bea Coninckx, Leo Dumon and Chris Van Wyngene work exclusively for the PGCB project (2.5 positions). This, at the same time, is a lot and very little — it is a lot that an institution is willing to grant 2.5 jobs for such a project, yet it is very little considering the task to be fulfilled. At the beginning, Els Coghe too had belonged to the team, but much to her regret, she was soon removed from the project and assigned to other tasks.

The premises of the project group are located above the laundry in an old and slightly shabby building. Steep stairs lead to the vast office that at the same time serves as therapy room. Next door some former workshops are used alternately for occupational therapy and for the project group.

The PGCB project provides the following services:
• *Individual therapy:* Individual sessions on the PGCB premises, one-to-one conversations within a group setting, individual therapy in groups, and individual therapy on the wards.
• *Group therapy:* Meeting groups, a contact-learning group, a Pre-Therapy group for people with mental disabilities.
• *A weekly informal meeting.*
• *Supervision, co-supervision and training* for nurses, occupational therapists etc.

1. Individual therapy

Individual sessions
These are offered at the PGCB premises for:
• patients of the whole institution who are referred for Pre-Therapy by the

psychiatrists;
• patients with whom it had been possible to have a dialogue and establish contact;
• patients for whom the group (or who for the group) would cause too much strain.

Their psychiatrists define individual therapy goals, and the therapists offer the patients a specific kind of therapeutic relationship which allows them to express their feelings and experiences. How this is realised depends completely on the individual possibilities and difficulties of each patient. The aim is to build up contact functions, to help patients to get in contact with their experiencing, but also to consciously perceive them in their own idiosyncratic way and to treat them more adequately. These are psychotic patients who are to some degree able to communicate and some of whom hear voices.

CARL is 32 years old and has been at the hospital since 1987. His history includes neglect, maltreatment, abuse, vagrancy, and prison.
   Before the Pre-Therapy programme existed there had been several attempts with different therapies for Carl that all failed. He could never keep to it, was almost constantly psychotic and extremely frightened. Since 1995, within the context of the project, he comes for individual therapy once a week. He never misses one single hour (whereas before he had not been able to keep to any therapy).
   At first Carl used to speak very briefly and superficially about something that had happened in his life without showing any feeling or sign of experiencing. After some months he started, very cautiously, to talk about his voices, calling them 'the little voices'. Introducing the voices opened new perspectives for the therapy. What he is expressing can now be talked through with the therapist in a quite different way, and step by step, he learns to deal with the voices instead of just being their victim. During this whole period he also regularly attends working therapy.
   Now and then he starts to question his symbolic language and to realise that it is not understandable for everybody. Slowly he begins to trust and admit his feelings and experiences. Sometimes he still uses psychotic symbolisations during the therapy sessions, but it happens less and less.
   The increasing progress in developing his identity is obvious. Carl thinks in a more realistic way about a future outside the hospital. He is able to take his own initiatives and, with a little support, to carry them through. He is actually preparing to move into a sheltered apartment outside the institution. He is still hearing voices, but is able to handle them better, and they no longer frighten him as much as before.

For the patients it is very important that this is a place where they can talk about their voices if they want to. This way they can learn to deal and cope with them. 'It is difficult to talk about voices in this institution,' the therapists explain. 'Patients are very reluctant to do so, because they are afraid of getting more medication then. When somebody talks about hearing voices, the usual response of the nurses is, "Just don't listen." In traditional training, nurses were taught to tell the patients not to listen to their voices. It is, so to speak, forbidden to talk about voices. Thus patients are trained to keep silent, because they don't want to appear even more crazy, and so their isolation gets increasingly worse. In individual therapy they may feel secure enough to talk about their voices.'

One-to-one conversations in a group setting

The Prouty Group I

This is a group for patients who are able to leave the ward. It takes place at the PGCB offices once a week. The contact abilities of these patients move between very basic forms of personal contact and simple verbal contacts. The therapists work mainly with Pre-Therapy in order to stimulate their existing capabilities and to develop contact. This group is above all about therapists and clients meeting each other. The main task of the therapists is to recognise, respond to and foster the patients' attempts for contact in whatever way they are expressed.

The patients are free to move around the different rooms, they may have coffee, listen to music, look at magazines, play, or, in the entrance room, smoke a cigarette. This specific open structure facilitates contact work. The patients are free to choose whatever they like to do and the team, in this relaxed atmosphere, has a good chance to reach them. A word about the taste of a cigarette or about always choosing the same favourite seat may initiate a short dialogue.

All three therapists are present. There is not a specific therapist responsible for a specific patient, but the three of them together are there for all of them. Sometimes a therapist addresses a person and, if there is no response, after a while one of the others might try again and perhaps succeed. This way the patients are offered contact by different persons. The patients are given time to warm up and the choice of getting different stimuli from different personalities.

For example on December 4, 1996: Some patients come by themselves, others are brought in by nurses. Some obviously have difficulties with the steep stairs. They spread out into the different rooms. Most of them first line up for the cigarettes that Leo is distributing. In the entrance hall where smoking is admitted there are some comfortable chairs. Inside, there is coffee available, magazines are displayed, music is played, and in the last room there is a TV.

The therapists go from one to the other and try to make contact. According to the person's reaction, a longer or shorter dialogue may ensue or the patient is left alone. Chris, who had been ill and could not join the group for three weeks, has longer conversations with some patients in the office.

As Bea approaches a patient, he points at me angrily, scolding: 'I don't know this one.' Bea explains to him who I am and what I am doing here. I sit down in the smoking room where Leo is starting to talk with some patients. He introduces me to Eric who in a faultless well-educated way says: 'Enchanté de faire votre connaissance, Madame.' I answer equally with, 'Enchantée,' and mention that we had seen each other from a distance yesterday on the ward. His eyes are shining. We have a few words together. Tom comes and asks Leo for a cigarette. But Leo dismisses him, explaining that right now he is talking with Eric. Tom asks me for a cigarette, but I don't have any, and we talk for a while in a French–English–Flemish gibberish. From time to time he says: 'Marlis-Tom', and I repeat: 'Marlis-Tom'. Our conversation makes Eric smile. Leo responds to that, and again a short dialogue develops between the two of them.

The team feels it is a great help to be three. If one of them does not get anywhere with a patient, the other might succeed. Or if one of them is successful this time, the other might be next time. They observe that, after a while, some patients choose one of them as their personal therapist

The Prouty Group II
This also takes place weekly at the premises of the project group. In this group, a more specific individual therapy setting has developed. The nine participants come together at the same time, but each one has an individual conversation with his personal therapist These conversations take place in a separate room. As a rule, they are shorter than regular individual therapy sessions, depending on how much the patient can cope with. With some of the patients a very intense personal and emotional contact is gradually developed.

MANUEL is 59 and has lived at the hospital since 1961. When the therapists started to practise Pre-Therapy with him on the ward, he reacted in a very disturbed way and seemed to feel even more insecure.

He uttered a wild torrent of words that were hard to follow. It was as if every word would immediately, and without any coherence, provoke the next one. Once, he suddenly jumped on the table when the therapist was addressing him and gave a passionate but completely incomprehensible speech.

After a few weeks the torrent of words diminished. Manuel no longer talked in this extremely associative manner, but started to express himself more coherently. He talked about more real issues, though still in a symbolic language code: 'I am like a lion flying out of his mouth, I made a hole and I cannot fix it anymore, there is a hook in the chain, when it breaks it's finished, my mind drops away, I gambled and lost, now I shall feel it, you want to put a point after it, but you can't find the point, it does not help to run away, you are tied to a spring...'

After a year his speech became quieter, less driven, less symbolically encoded. He started to come to the rooms of the project group although not regularly, as he often fell back into old behaviour patterns, and when he did not come, Chris went to see him on the ward. However, he now talked about issues like getting old, looking back on a life that had not been as he had wished it to be (no work, no wife, no children), about regrets, fears of further declining (physically and psychologically), missing relations and family. Now he sometimes can stop talking and wait, and from time to time more pleasant memories are coming up, he thinks of suicide less often, too.

Manuel now participates in the Prouty Group II, with Chris Van Wyngenen as his personal therapist

Some patients want to talk as a priority about everyday life on the ward.

For JAN this is the only place where he talks about himself. He speaks in a very slow and whispering voice which is hard to understand. During the week, on the ward, he tries from time to time to say something, but as listening to him is so difficult and tiring, scarcely anybody has the time and patience to do so. Music is another way to make contact with him. The project group has a small synthesizer; Bea plays songs·that he knows and so contact may develop through music. Lately he also speaks about his father, his adolescence and even his voices. Slowly the contact becomes more personal.

Wherever possible the therapists try to pick up what they perceive as little contact points. To have a point of reference makes contact much easier for the patients.

RALF in former years used to paint and was really good at it. His father had been curator of a museum. From time to time the therapists ask him if he would like to do some painting again. So far he has always said no, but perhaps one day he will want to. They just want him to know that the opportunity is there. Once, when Ralf saw the video camera he suddenly remembered that in former times he used to take pictures.

These are contact moments, and with time they happen more often and more quickly. Even when these moments do not go further they break the isolation of the patients and thus improve the quality of their lives.

In addition to the one-to-one conversations, there is an open space for the patients to chat, play or listen to music. These opportunities are left over from the time when the aim had been to activate patients. They are still there, but it is entirely up to the patients whether they make use of them. The more personal the contact that develops, the less the need for these things. Opportunities for specific activities are now more and more taken up on the ward itself. Here, if they want, they can just sit around or smoke a cigarette. Only rarely do the patients get in contact with each other. As their contact functions are severely impaired, this is too difficult for them.

Individual therapy on the ward
To those patients for whom Client-Centred Psychotherapy is indicated, but who are not able to leave the ward and come to the therapy rooms, individual therapy if offered on the ward. The therapists go to different wards and meet

the patients wherever they are.

For example on December 3, on the ward St Aloysius: Leo Dumon takes me there and *Hans Chielens* joins us for translation. In a big living room a television is running, and there are cosy chairs. A number of men shuffle along or sit around apathetically; some watch television, others just stare, each one is by himself.

ALBERT is sitting bent forward in a chair on which he is, because of his epilepsy, tied with a broad textile belt. He is leafing through a magazine, hastily, mechanically and, it seems, without taking anything in. Each time he gets to the end, he starts anew from the beginning. Leo sits down next to him and reflects the situation, 'Albert looks at the magazine', 'Albert is leafing through the magazine'. Leo points to the printed text: 'Albert is reading', or to a picture, 'There is a car', etc. Albert does not show any reaction. Only once, when Leo is pointing to a page, he vehemently turns it and looks at the next one. After a while Leo says: 'We stop now, I shall be back next Tuesday and then I bring you a magazine.' Albert nods.

Leo states that today Albert was much less approachable than usual. Perhaps he is angry because Leo forgot to bring a new magazine as he usually does? Or perhaps he was irritated by my presence? Leo goes to his next client, an old man who is slumped in a chair, a bit away from the television set.

BERNARD had only recently been transferred from another ward. Leo asks him how he likes it here. He likes it, he likes the food, especially the meat, but there are no cigarettes, he doesn't like that. Leo rolls him a cigarette and explains that today he didn't bring cigarettes with him, only tobacco, and therefore has to roll one for Bernard. Bernard begins to tell Leo about bicycle tubes that his father used to repair and about how much it cost and that nowadays it is much more expensive. He talks about the grave of his parents. He has never seen it, but his brothers and sisters have described it to him. He would like to see where his parents are buried. He is unhappy that he had never been taken to the cemetery. His mother, not his sister, will come and visit him. The sister always tells him to shake hands.

From time to time his cigarette goes out, and Leo has to give him a light. Leo talks quite a while with Bernard. Then he shakes his hand, promising to be back next week.

Jeanine Carels, the ward's head nurse, is around and attentively watches Leo working. From time to time she sits down too next to a patient trying to begin a short conversation. Afterwards, when we have coffee together, Hans Chielens expresses his surprise about Bernard talking so much and even shaking hands with Leo. Hans knows Bernard from the other ward and has not seen him for a while. He says that there, Bernhard had not talked at all and not wanted to be touched. Each bath had been a fight. Jeanine says that they don't have a problem here with Bernard taking a bath or a shower. They talk with to him and explain him, step by step, what is happening.

My impression is, that on this ward the project group's way of working has influenced how the staff deal with the patients in everyday routine. In Luc Roelens' opinion it is relevant too that for many patients tension releases when they are admitted to a ward like St Aloysius, which probably has a stronger tradition in medical nursing than other wards, where 'activation' of the patients still is the main concern.

In the beginning, when there had been four in the project group, two therapists always worked together in a ward. The example of Fernand described below shows how useful this can be. But nowadays therapists miss this advantage as they have to work by themselves. There is just one ward, St Dymfna, where Bea Coninckx and Leo Dumon still work together.

For example on December 12, 1996: On this ward the therapists have two rooms at their disposal where they can be alone with the clients: the TV room, which is closed to patients during the day, and a small office separated from the workshop by a glass screen. At the workshop some men are doing handicraft work; others just sit there, doze or walk around. Despite the separate rooms it is impossible to have real privacy. Patients who have seen Bea through the glass screen come in and ask her questions. The nurses too, every now and then, have something to do in the office.

Bea's first client today is . . .

. . . ERNESTO, a lively younger man (around 30). Despite his unkempt appearance, he is visibly better dressed than most of the other men here. Ernesto comes from a wealthy family who lives in Spain for six months a year. He talks a lot and hastily tells her that his parents are in Spain but that his father will soon be coming for his birthday. He asserts that he will try to be good to the others and learn from them so that they will like him. He cannot stop talking and Bea has a hard time ending the conversation after twenty minutes.

In a later conversation the PGCB team point to how clearly this short episode indicates the progress Ernesto has made. He is now more able to accept structures and contact boundaries. This is also observable at the informal meetings in which he regularly participates. Luc Roelens had known Ernesto for many years before the therapist started to work with him; he is amazed to see the progress he has made.

Bea had already told me about her next patient:

FERNAND, aged 71, has been in the hospital since 1955. The nursing staff had warned Bea that on the ward he was considered dangerous and violent. However, in the living room he readily allowed Bea to sit next to him and immediately started to tell her about his religiously shaped hallucinatory world (being God, having to sacrifice himself and save the world). From time to time he interwove episodes and experiences from his childhood into the narrative, and when there was a break, he filled it by singing. At first he was singing by himself; later Bea began to join in. This offered a new, quite realistic opportunity for contact: Fernand brought his song book and showed her which songs he wanted to sing with her.

Then more and more memories emerged in which he associated external facts with what he experienced. He explained how he had worked for different organisations and had always wanted to be perfect in everything he was doing. He talked about his ambiguous relations with girls, and how he had wished to get married. He also described the emotional rupture with his family, particularly his father, and that his admission to the hospital provoked.

After some time, he no longer wanted to talk with Bea in the living room where other patients were present, but wanted to have more privacy.

He expressed himself now in a less psychotic way and introduced very existential issues (getting old and increasingly declining, death coming nearer, not having lived, and about his fears concerning sexuality).

One day he suddenly no longer wanted Bea as his therapist He probably felt he had told her too much. In his language she had seduced him to sin. Leo took over, and for some time Fernand fell back into his former psychotic ways of expressing himself.

Then, slowly, he accepted that Bea occasionally made contact again. Eventually Bea took over again, and Fernand picked up therapy exactly at the point where he had left it. Obviously it had been unbearable for him to get through his psychotic relapse with Bea. For the time being he needed somebody else, until he came back to the point where he had got stuck with her.

As we come to the ward, Fernand is sitting asleep on a bench near the window. Bea asks him if he would rather sleep or talk with her. He wants to talk and follows her to the office. Bea remarks that he is wearing a new hat.

FERNAND points to two black patches on the hat and says, 'These are my sins.' He adds that he has to be good and do everything right in order to get rid of his sins. Then he speaks about how in the past he had worked as a 'propagandist', recruiting members for the Christian Workers' youth organisation. He talks about heaven and about how he has to be absolutely perfect in everything he does.

The pressure of a rigid religious education, and the taboocd sexuality behind these confused ideas, are clearly recognisable. Bea gently tries to suggest that being perfect in everything is impossible and trying one's best is enough. When after a while he no longer feels like talking, he starts a song they sing together.

During coffee break we sit with the nurses and the cleaning team. About 40 patients have coffee next door; it is very noisy, and every now and then one of the staff has to go and see if everything is all right. The mood is very different from when I was there two days earlier (see pp. 146–8). There are more patients and some other nurses, and the atmosphere is tougher. There is a certain tension and nervousness in the air, especially when Bea mentions a patient who had been aggressive and was punished by being forbidden to leave the ward for four weeks. She is obviously outraged about somebody getting punished for a behaviour caused by illness.

After the break I join Leo in the TV room, where he is talking with one of his clients. Today the door cannot be locked, because the lock is broken. Every now and then other patients come in and are kindly, but firmly, dismissed by Leo.

> PAUL, about 50, who has been at the hospital for 15 years, looks sad and depressed. He talks about his family. He misses them terribly, on the weekend they will come and visit him. He is irritated by the noise. More than other patients he is aware of, and reacts to, what is going on around him. He also has a few words with me.

Working on the wards is very demanding for the three therapists. It is not easy, in that setting, to carefully listen to the patients who often speak in a very low and indistinct voice. Several times the therapist is interrupted by nurses wanting something, by other patients interfering, having a question or asking for a cigarette. Constantly, while talking with a patient, they briefly and patiently respond to somebody else, even if only to explain that they don't have time to talk to them just then.

Originally the intention had been to have the one-to-one conversations on the wards together with the nurses, so that they too might find a better approach to the patients and respond to them differently. With some nurses this went very well: they were open to new ideas for their work and able to integrate some into their daily routine. These nurses managed to meet two contradictory demands: on the one hand to respond to and understand the patients, and on the other having to make demands and to set boundaries. Yet many nurses were not willing to try this new way of working and with them co-operation is often quite difficult. Some felt that they just have to take care of the patients and don't understand why they should sit and talk with and listen to them. Some wards refuse to co-operate with the project group, and no approach is possible. 'To change mentalities is very difficult, we know that from ourselves,' says Chris Van Wyngene, 'it is necessary also to give oneself serious thoughts, and not everybody wants to do that.'

However, those nurses who committed themselves to it, declared that serious self-exploration proved to be rewarding and had positive effects not only for the patients, but for themselves as well.

2. Group therapy

Meeting groups
These groups offer the patients an opportunity to talk about their concerns. With the necessary consideration of discretion and safety, they are encouraged to communicate with each other. It is not a matter of sophisticated encounter group, just of quite normal forms of being together. There are two such groups, and for each there is one therapist responsible.

Chris Van Wyngene describes his group:
'They come together for an hour, and we talk about whatever they want. Whatever they like to do — read, have coffee — it is their hour where they can do what they want. This is a big difference compared with other activities, where they always have to do something. Here they can decide themselves how they want to spend their time. There is a certain amount of interaction. They talk with each other, tell about their plans for the weekend, if they will be going home, report things from the ward, talk about the nurses. They all come from different wards. This is important because it offers them an opportunity to meet other people, to make friends. There is a break from June to September — but after that they always want to come back, they like it.'

In Leo Dumon's group conversation is more focused:
'The patients tell one after the other what at the moment they are concerned about, and then we talk it through. They come for three years now, and they too want to continue. It is not a highly sophisticated therapy group, but depending on how they feel at the moment, they ask questions. One patient, for example, is concerned about what to do when his mother dies. He does not talk with anybody else about it, but he is worried about what then will become of him. They do talk about personal concerns, sometimes, not always. Sometimes they have problems with each other. But if they have difficulties with another participant, they do not dare to tell him directly, but mention it first to me. Sometimes it is just having coffee or talking about soccer, it depends.'

The contact learning group
This is a group for patients who show some kind of contact initiatives that in daily life are not given sufficient attention or responded to. The patients are offered individual approaches within the setting of a small group, and at the same time the therapists aim at encouraging spontaneous interaction attempts between the patients. They work a lot with Pre-Therapy. The therapists address each patient individually, one after the other, and when there is contact, help to develop it further. Usually contact first happens through the therapist, who then tries to facilitate interaction between the participants themselves. It is not a specific therapy group, but above all, a matter of making contact here and then.

ADRIAN was born in 1930 and had been at the hospital since 1956. He used to live in a strictly closed ward, was aggressive, suffered from hallucinations, and showed very bizarre behaviours. He had a strict day programme which included working therapy and movement therapy, and he did everything docilely, indifferently, without resistance — a good patient, quite 'crazy' though, but a good patient. The nurses of the ward could not understand why this man should join the contact learning group. He was working well and didn't cause any problems. They were afraid that in the group he would become even more psychotic.

'Of course, when people develop contact, they often get in contact with their psychotic parts too', the therapists agree, ' but we can handle that.' At the beginning it was difficult to talk with Adrian. His language was very psychotic and turned around confused religious and paranoid issues. With time, he slowly became more personal, more connected with reality, more active, and was developing in a very positive way.

When he was to be transferred to a sheltered apartment, he used the group for dealing with all the questions, wishes, experiences and considerations this change brought up for him. He also expressed his anger — 'Why do they do that now? Why not thirty years ago? — and he talked about his fears and about difficulties with his fellow residents. The therapists contacted the relevant team. Some problems could be resolved and some of his wishes met. Slowly he began to feel at home in the community. Later he decided to leave the contact-learning group, because on the same weekday there was a market in his village, and he wanted to go there with his friend. On his birthday he invited the therapists for coffee and told them about his decision — at the same time inviting them for his next birthday.

Pre-Therapy group for people with mental disabilities
The Pre-Therapy group is a small group for people with both mental impairment and psychological problems, in which six people participate. One is psychotic, another very depressive, some are completely apathetic and had barely any contact with the group or only in a very impersonal way, and one patient shows pronounced autistic behaviour.

The therapists look for signs of contact or relation that they could take up. They try to make contact with each person in turn. With one patient they work exclusively with Pre-Therapy, with another it is more of a conversation. And when contact begins to develop, they try to foster interaction.

PIETER, born in 1966 with Down's Syndrome, came to Sint-Amandus in 1993. He was very withdrawn and depressive. He went to working therapy, but remained completely passive and indifferent. He did not talk, did not want to join the others for a vacation, sat in the same corner all the time, withdrawing more and more into himself.

The carers turned to the project group for help. Leo immediately had contact with Pieter, and very soon a solid relationship was established. Pieter began to make sounds — at first just whispering, then with full voice. Now he seems to be more aware of the others in the group, he responds more when somebody address him, and sometimes he spontaneously addresses somebody himself. He talks about his experiences and feelings, how he is longing for his parents and afraid of the people here. Before, he had lived with his parents, and it was a shock for him to be moved to the clinic were everything is so different. At home he had sometimes been aggressive, and Leo thinks Pieter might believe that he was brought here to be punished. He often says that he is sad, and that he likes Leo.

Two years ago Leo went for a holiday with Pieter's group. The carers were very concerned about how it would go with Pieter. It went very well. Since then Pieter has no problems joining the others, whereas before this had been absolutely impossible for him.

This example once more shows that a client-centred approach such as Pre-Therapy can be useful for a person with mental impairment. This had not been assumed and is still not fully recognised in Beernem. The Pre-Therapy project was originally intended only for psychotic patients but fortunately the project group did not stick too closely to this restriction.

Karen Neyt, carer at St Pieters, a ward for people with mental disabilities, sent me a written report of an example of how Pre-Therapy had not only positive effects on the client but also on the people around him.

RAOUL: 'A few years ago he was completely withdrawn in himself, had no contact with the team or with the group. When we tried to make contact with him, it remained a rather one-sided thing. It took a long time before Raoul showed any reaction. We had to repeat a question at least five times before getting an answer, if we got one at all.

'Raoul was very mistrusting and suspicious. He observed everything around him, not taking his eyes off people and things. He was always afraid of being robbed, but he could not be trusted either, as he was stealing from others himself. He never joined the group, just hanging around in the hall and trying to keep an eye on everything. Probably there was much more going on in Raoul than he was able to express. People who saw him for the first time underestimated him. He was admitted to Pre-Therapy.

'Now his contact behaviour has completely changed. He is sitting together with us, quite relaxed, and spontaneously talking about this and that. He often joins the others and participates in the activities of the ward. Sometimes he gets up in the night to say hello to the night staff.

'Raoul is still suspicious, but to some extent he, as well as the group and the staff, can live with that. This is also because many things are now clearer to him. We learned that things need to be made much clearer to him.

Sometimes the therapists go to see a member of the Pre-Therapy group on the ward. As I said, 'There is much more going on in Raoul than as been able to express'.

For example on December 4th, 1996: Leo Dumon takes me to see Pieter at the Holy Heart Ward. Anita Hillewaere, the head carer, takes us to a spacious, well-lit room, that looks more colourful and serene than the rooms I have seen before at the other wards. People with mental disabilities sit at different tables doing some kind of handicraft work.

PIETER plays with little pieces of paper. Leo speaks to him, pointing to the pieces, and a little play goes on between them; alternately they point with the finger to one of the papers. After that they sing together. Pieter is very affectionate, and wants to hug and kiss Leo — a little too much for Leo. Pieter lays his head on Leo's shoulder, Leo strokes him and then says goodbye.

In the meantime another young man, also with Down's Syndrome, tries to get my attention by making noises with his lips. This would be a good opportunity to make contact by picking up the movement of his lips. But not wanting to interrupt Leo's interaction with Pieter, I don't pay attention to the young man. After a while the sounds become louder, then they get stereotypical, and the man turns away. Very distinctly different nuances were visible in his behaviour; what at first had been a shy attempt at contact, turned into a stereotyped tic as there was no response.

Anita Hillewaere shows me the bedrooms (with up to eight beds), everything looks very hospital-like. At least there are some personal items above each bed. 'We do what we can to make it a little cosy,' Anita says. She has worked here for many years and is happy, that many things have changed for the better.

3. *The informal meeting*

The informal meeting takes place every Friday afternoon for two hours and is open to all patients of the hospital. Everybody who wants to come is welcome. It is meant to be a place where patients are listened to and have an opportunity to informally meet patients of other wards, a very normal meeting place. They can have coffee and do whatever they want. Usually there are about 20 people and sometimes they bring somebody with them. All three therapists are present. The patients come and go just as they like. There are no rules, except that a minimal respecting of social norms is expected.

ERNESTO (see p. 132) was born in 1962 and had been at the clinic for fifteen years. He is mentally disabled and suffers from epilepsy. He makes a huge effort trying to live above his capabilities. Therefore his behaviour on the ward is very tense and intrusive and he tries to take as much attention as he can get. But at the meetings, however, the therapists observe that he can also let go of his usual demands, and be patient and relaxed with other patients.

Problems too are brought up in this setting, for example if there are difficulties on a ward. For the patients it is a safe place where they can talk without fear about all these things. Sometimes the result of a conversation started here is that the patient takes up psychotherapy. This is another important aspect of the informal group: the patients get an idea of what therapy might be and can decide if they want it. Moreover, the meeting is a concrete opportunity to establish reality contact. Outside the hospital it is a quite normal situation that people who know each other meet and talk together. The informal meeting on Friday afternoon is offering these contact-impaired people some of this aspect of reality.

However, the patients are not really free to come to the meeting. They are dependent on the ward letting them go. And sometimes when somebody has been transferred to another ward it might get difficult. It depends very much on the goodwill and the attitude of the staff, and also on what they have heard about the meeting, and from whom.

The team of the project group wishes they could organise a room for the patients where they could meet without the therapists: 'A place where everybody could come to and where they could do whatever they want. A place that would be *their* place. The informal meeting is a step in this direction. But as the staff are present it is declared as therapy, and so they can come. It needs this label. But to meet each other could in itself be very therapeutic.' Their dream is to have a place that would be open for the patients daily, where they could come to breathe, for half an hour or perhaps just for five minutes. 'It would be *their* place, for which they would be responsible themselves. We would not be present, or just sometimes, but usually not, it should be a room *for them,*' say the three therapists, knowing full well that it is unlikely to be possible. However, they like the idea of a place where there would be no control. And they are convinced that the patients would deal with a room of their own in a very responsible way.

Taking responsibility for oneself is an important aspect of reality contact. As the patients, in many areas, are not able to take this responsibility, in institutions there is a tendency not to believe them capable of any at all. Yet to take all responsibilities away from them reinforces the patients' disintegration and sometimes may even promote it.

Summarising their work with the patients, the project group states: 'Within the PGCB project we have to work with chronic psychiatric patients whose contact functions are impaired. We observe that when we meet the patients with a client-centred attitude, elementary forms of contact become possible and simple conversations are developing. With some patients it does not go further, but the relationship that has been established is breaking up their isolation and improving the quality of their life. Others can take further steps and working on their problems becomes possible.'

And they let me have a glimpse into their statistics: in May 1996 they worked with 116 patients, of these there were 17 people in individual therapy, 28 in individual therapy within a group setting, 45 in individual therapy on the ward, 14 in group therapy and 33 persons at the informal meeting.

4. Supervision and training

Supervision and training for nurses, occupational and working therapists etc. is another task of the project group; at the beginning it had remained somewhat in the background. On the wish of the nursing management, this aspect will be given more importance in the future.

The manager of the nursing department manager, *Emmanuel Langerock*, thinks that developing contact with the patients must be a basic task of the nurses. A broader spreading of Prouty's approach is more important to him than intense therapeutic work with just a few patients. He would like more nurses to participate in innovations, even if then those might be more modest He thinks that in the beginning the project had been pushed too much, and the reservations of the nurses not sufficiently taken into consideration.

It is certainly true that the nurses have the most opportunities for understanding the patients in their individual ways and responding to them. And it is extremely desirable for Prouty's approach that a basic client-centred attitude — and that is actually what was first intended — should be increasingly adopted by the nurses. However, the value of individual therapeutic work should not be underestimated either. The therapists — coming from the outside and not having a direct function within the ward — have other opportunities to relate to the patients and with them other areas may open up than do so in daily life. Psychotherapy and person-centred care on the ward should complement each other. Yet, there are limits to what the three therapists can manage.

From 1997 onwards the main focus of the project group was to pass on their experience to the nurses and to offer training in client-centred ways of working and supervision. This meant that the therapists had less time for the patients, and at first they were not at all happy about it. Though they agree that supervision and training are very important, they had, at the time of my visit, mixed feelings about the coming changes. They were afraid that a majority of the staff would not be really interested in this training, and they were worried about having less time to help the patients.

As a matter of fact, the nurses too want to do something for the patients, but have other ideas of what that should be. Some staff members do not fully understand the work of the project group. 'Other therapeutic programmes where the patients 'do' something are taken much more seriously,' is the therapists' impression. 'Somebody just sitting there for fifty minutes talking about his feelings, does not count for them. Activities are much more valued; for example, when somebody goes to working therapy, this counts. Yet, we observe again and again that patients are much more willing to participate in activities when we first succeed in making contact with them.' It happens quite frequently that a patient does not come to the therapy session because he is participating in another activity that is considered more important by the nurses.

'This is our problem: we achieve something with a person — but then it does not count at all. In their view, we do just nothing,' the therapists complain. But they also admit that perhaps they had sometimes demanded too much and not sufficiently considered the situation of the nurses. They are willing to give their thoughts on how to handle this differently and to take more into account the nurses' frame of reference.

The PGCB team has now developed and introduced a training programme for the staff. In March 2001 they wrote to me:

'Having finished our third training programme, we see a different attitude toward Pre-Therapy and client-centred working on the different wards. There is a more open attitude toward the needs of the clients; they have some freedom for making their own choices. But individual process thinking still remains difficult. The focus remains on the group as therapy unit. For the trainees, to integrate Pre-Therapy and client-centred thinking in their daily work is still unusual. They stand alone with this approach; it would be better if the philosophy of the ward would correspond more.'

Pre-therapeutic approaches on the wards

Even though it had not been possible to introduce the person-centred attitude and pre-therapeutic ways of working in the whole field of nursing as extensively as Luc Roelens had hoped, there are some remarkable attempts proving their worth, that hopefully, with time, will spread out more. These attempts are to the credit of some open-minded and committed staff members for whom meeting Prouty and his Pre-Therapy lead to considerable changes in their way of working.

1. Pre-Therapy in the field of nursing
Anne Degadt, nurse on the ward St Cornelius, reports:

'Before Prouty, I had seen, for example, Michael as a very easy patient. He washed and shaved himself, was always on time, never aggressive. He was anxious and afraid of contact, did not ask for much attention and cause no trouble. After Prouty, I realised, that I just took care of Michael, but did not really know who he was and what was going on in him. Nor did I know that of most of the other patients. Before Prouty, I called the patients' behaviours bizarre, disturbed or problematic, without thinking about the reasons of this behaviour or about methods how to deal with them. After Prouty, I tried to change my attitude. For example: there was a patient who in the kitchen was incessantly walking around in circles. Before, I would have told him to stop. Now, I walked with him for a while and he took this quite naturally and explained me why he was doing it. All at once there was contact.

'And each time I met Michael, who never said anything and ran away when he saw me, I now said: 'Michael'. And after a while he stopped when he saw me. And soon I could sit next to him or walk with him without him running away.'

At bedtime, Anne Degadt regularly spent a little time with Michael, sat on his bedside and tried to reflect what she perceived around him. This way more and more contact became possible.

'By trial and error,' says Anne. 'If he pulled the blanket over his head when I came to his room, I knew that it would be difficult. When he said: "I knew that you would come," he had been waiting for me, and it was easier to make contact. He talked about things that had happened during the day — a visit, a new shirt. But sometimes he also said amazing things about what he experienced and how lonely he felt. Things that he would never have been able to say three years ago.'

It visibly bothers her deeply that he had been transferred to another ward and she lost touch with him. Koen Vanquaethem has joined our conversation. He works as a psychological assistant at St Jan Berchmans, the ward Michael has been transferred to and where they work with a new concept based on humanistic psychology. Yet, though the transfer actually represents an improvement, Michael reacted by relapsing. Koen tells us that again he is totally withdrawn, does not want Anne to visit him and has no contact with anybody on the ward. He reassures Anne that Michael is met with the necessary understanding and patience to help him get used to his new life. Yet, the relapse certainly could have been avoided or at least moderated if he had been informed of and prepared for this move. It is a shame when a patient is set back this way, by administrative measures that — at least temporarily — destroy the long-term patient work of a committed nurse. For the sake of everybody involved such impediments should be avoided whenever possible.

Often it's not the move itself which is the problem (sometimes for the patient it even represents an improvement), but the way it is done. A patient is told, without any previous warning, that today he has to move. He is given no time to prepare for this change. Suddenly he has to leave the milieu he was used to, and the people he knows, and has to cope with new circumstances and new people. Any contact which has been built up is suddenly torn away. The patients do not understand why this is done to them and often believe that they are being punished. The consequences are withdrawal, deterioration or increasing aggression. Often the nurses too get very short notice of the planned change. And more than once, the therapists of the project group were not informed at all that one of their patients had been moved and they are not even given a chance to say goodbye.

Yet therapists or nurses who have already developed contact with a patient would be the right people to prepare them for a forthcoming change and to respond to their questions, fears and reservations. Therefore they should be informed at an early stage, and the patients should be given enough time to deal with the changes to come. Certainly, with a little bit of planning and good will, this could easily be realised. The extra effort involved would be repaid by avoiding many problems, backlashes and aggressions. The new start at a new place would be much easier, not only for the patients, but also for the nurses. However, it could be difficult to persuade those in authority that a preparatory period adjusted to the rhythm of a patient with psychological problems is necessary and ultimately to the advantage of everybody involved. The more remote from the patients the decision-makers are, the less they will know about their reality.

To make decisions about patients without informing them, assuming that they will not understand, completely contradicts a humanistic point of view. This is equally true for the concept of punishment — a relic still existing in psychiatry which harks back to the times when psychiatric institutions used to be prisons. Bea Coninckx is right to be upset when an aggressive patient is punished by not being allowed to leave the ward for four weeks. Of course, aggression cannot be tolerated — there must be consequences, nurses and other patients have to be protected — but the measures taken should make sense and be comprehensible to the patients. They have to be related to the misbehaviour and help to diminish it. But many nurses feel it is too much effort to have to find individual solutions for the specific situation. They are afraid of not being able to justify it to the other patients and of losing control, when there are no clearly defined sanctions they can fall back on.

A bit of understanding of how the patient might feel is often the best way to prevent aggressive outbursts. 'Many aggressions are stimulated by trying to oppress them. If the nurses instead reflect how the patients feel — angry, upset, hurt — they feel understood and accepted, and usually calm down very quickly', is the PGCB team's experience. But many nurses cannot see that as a good option, particularly since they are under constant pressure of time. However, to respond in time to the looming bad moods of a patient, in the end, costs much less time than having to deal with his aggressions. It is again a matter of a shift in thinking that at first might seem difficult, but will result in considerable improvements for the nurses. Therefore this shift is an essential aspect of training and supervision where the nurses should be helped to develop practical alternatives and reduce anxieties.

With all the patients who have had Pre-Therapy, considerable changes could be observed. This is documented by a — by now substantial — collection of video tapes. I watched a number of them and was repeatedly impressed to see how patients, who for years, or even decades, had not been able to express themselves, gradually developed abilities to communicate.

At St Dymfna I saw a video showing different periods of long-term individual pre-therapeutic work of the head nurse *Johan De Brabander* with a completely withdrawn patient. It is remarkable how he slowly, carefully and empathetically establishes contact. The patient's transformation from somebody who barely showed any reaction into a merrily chatting man is just amazing.

Marie-Jeanne Hudders too presents two video tapes of her pre-therapeutic work with a patient of St Cornelius.

ARNO always runs away when somebody is approaching him, as seen on the first video tape from 1989, the year Prouty came to Beernem. After that, Marie-Jeanne started to work with Arno. At first nothing was possible, he did not let her approach him. In a meeting it was suggested that she should pay attention to the little things that in daily life meant something to him, and try to start from there. Marie-Jeanne began to spoil Arno, for example by preparing him a nice warm bath that he visibly enjoyed. She observed that Arno's shoes were not good any more, and as he liked to walk outside, she bought him a pair of solid warm shoes and warm underwear. She observed him at meals. They were six at table, and when the others sometimes took all the food without leaving something for Arno, he never asked for fresh supplies, but just did not eat. Marie-Jeanne started to ask him if he wanted more, and helped him to open the butter and jam wrappings.

'At first it was just very little, but with time he seemed to enjoy certain moments,' Marie-Jeanne recalls. 'Somehow I felt as if he would use me like a cosy piece of furniture. We did not really have contact, but I observed that things were easier for him when I was there. He smiled and knew my name, and after a while I could talk with him.'

Such conversations are recorded on the second video tape. Gradually Marie-Jeanne learned things about Arno, for example that he would like to go to church, but did not go because he had no suit. Marie-Jeanne provided a suit for him, so he could go to church again; all these small steps in daily life gradually became possible and improved the quality of his life.

'Arno opened up towards others too. It was as if a light had gone on. Before, he just existed, ate, slept, worked, but then he changed. Unfortunately I had the same "happy ending" as Anne had with Michael — Arno was moved to another ward,' is Marie-Jeanne Hudders' bitter closure.

Arno's example shows how special 'sessions' are not always needed for working with Pre-Therapy. Sometimes they are not even possible, and better starting points for making contact can be found in daily life. Thus Marie-Jeanne Hudders discovered that everything that happens around the bath is very important for the patients. For many of them it is connected with fears of slipping on a piece of soap, of falling and plunging into death. Marie-Jeanne takes that into consideration: she talks with the patients, takes care that the water is really warm and helps them to dry themselves properly. Usually everything has to go very quickly so that the patients often are still wet when they get dressed. Marie-Jeanne tries to ensure that the bath loses its terror: 'The patients enjoy it. And it does not take much more time. Though it is not possible with everybody, some patients don't want it. '

Anne Degadt and Marie-Jeanne Hudders explain, 'It is much more satisfying to work this way, it is a challenge. But sometimes it is very difficult, because some of our colleagues still do not understand or even disapprove of what we are doing'. They work on the same ward, but at different times, and they both feel a little isolated there.

Another problem is that some people are not even aware of the positive changes that the two nurses describe. Often what has not been achieved are the only things that are noticed — if a patient still has to be washed, still needs care, still is not able to work, then, in the opinion of some people, nothing has changed. They do not value other aspects, for example that a patient, who before just had walked through the ward shouting 'bumbumbum' and did not let anybody get near him, now accepts the therapist sitting next to him for half an hour and even sometimes touches his arm. But as small as these changes might appear, they are significant and might lead to further steps of growth if they are acknowledged and encouraged. An essential part in training and education of nurses should be the sensitising of their perception for such small but crucial steps of growth.

'Nurses are often afraid of patients getting aggressive,' explains Bea Coninckx who describes another difficulty: 'If a patient once had hit somebody — even if it is twenty years ago — they expect that any time he could do it again. He never gets rid of that stigma. It does not count that for twenty years nothing has happened.' Labels stick and impede change and improvement.

Sometimes, the members of the project group catch themselves having the heretical idea that destroying all the patients' notes would allow them a completely new start. They are convinced that many problems could be avoided if, from the beginning, patients would be taken more seriously. They think that then perhaps patients would be less likely to develop — in addition to the disorders they came with — more severe disorders as a result of being in the hospital. Accepting patients as they are facilitates their learning to live with their problems in a way that is socially acceptable. 'Yet this attitude requires professionals to be "real people". This might be frightening, but also gives oneself a good feeling. Once people have begun to work this way, they cannot draw back anymore. It is a different way of thinking,' says the project group.

It is this shift in thinking which for some staff members is so difficult. They are not able to reconcile it with the daily routine. And there is no doubt that the nurses' work is difficult and demanding, sometimes challenging them to their limits. This is not always sufficiently acknowledged. There is usually too few staff for too many patients who sometimes are very difficult and have to live together in very confined spaces. Nurses are constantly under pressure of time, everything has to be done quickly. On the other hand it happens frequently that two nurses, taking a patient to the toilet, talk to each other instead of to him. A nurse can also, by hiding behind the undisputed demands of everyday routine, neglect many an opportunity that actually would be there.

It needs a growth process for nurses to realise that building up contact with patients is not just work, but an essential part of their task, and that Prouty's contact reflections can easily be integrated into daily routine. Hopefully supervision and training will foster this process which in some places has already started.

I have seen on two quite different wards (St Dymfna and St Jan-

Berchmans), how knowing about Prouty's concepts has influenced staff who do not explicitly work with Pre-Therapy yet try increasingly to put into practice a person-centred attitude.

2. A day at St Dymfna

St Dymfna is a closed ward with the reputation of being very problematic. It is a big ward with 60 patients, among them a few extremely difficult personalities dominating the ward. When they are all together, there are always problems. In order to somehow improve matters, a 'stimulation and contact group' (Dymfna Animatie en Kontakt Groep) has been created, offering the severely disabled chronic patients different interpersonal activities. Between ten and twelve patients belong to this group (the number varies as participation is voluntary), for the most part elderly men who are no longer able to work and who previously had mostly been left to their own devices. Most of them are diagnosed schizophrenic, some suffer from organic brain damage, and also one of the last patients to have undergone a lobotomy belongs to the group. 'They are easy to get along with,' declares Johan De Brabander, 'though some of them can become quite aggressive. But it makes a big difference that they are no longer left to themselves, sitting around and not doing anything.'

During my day-long visit I get to see the different activities they offer to this group. First thing in the morning they have movement training, offered twice a week by the movement therapist, *Eric Buyck*. It is not a matter of performance, but much more of playfully doing something together. Eric is deeply impressed by Prouty. 'Since Prouty, I respond to the patients differently,' he says. 'For example, there is this man who each time, during the training, wants to go to the toilet. Before, I used to say, "You can't go now, you can go later". Now I say, "Okay, but you have to be back in ten minutes." The patient always punctually keeps to it, sometimes he is even back before the ten minutes are over.'

Today, as an exception due to my visit, the patients are brought to the sports complex by bus — normally they have to walk. As some of them suffer from minor physical disabilities, the walk takes them about fifteen minutes. That they make this effort twice a week proves that they really like the movement training. However, today they obviously enjoy being given a ride. Johan De Brabander and two other nurses join in, *Christine Adriaensens* and *Philippe Veys*.

At the gym, Eric Buyck gets them to do simple exercises, such as throwing rings on different posts. The farther away the posts, the more difficult it gets. Then it works the other way round: the rings have to be thrown on the same post, but each time the person throwing the ring has to take a step back, so that the distance grows bigger. They all manage the first throws, but then it becomes more difficult. Some patients must be encouraged to try it; others cannot wait their turn. Each patient's throw is approved. The nurses participate too, and their performances are neither better nor worse than those of the patients. The atmosphere is relaxed. At the end, those who did best get applause.

Back on the ward, the patients have a coffee break. Johan De Brabander talks to a younger man who is sitting bent forward in a chair, monotonously rocking. The man shakes his head. Johan explains me that he usually joins the group but today did not want to come. There is coffee for us too at the TV room, where I get to see several videos, among them the pre-therapeutic individual work of Johan de Brabander mentioned on p. 143.

We are joined now by *Marijke Magerman* and *Frank Verstraete* who also work with this group of patients. Frank Verstraete is an occupational therapist who gives the patients very simple individually designed tasks to fulfil. To Frank it is important that the patients know what they are doing so they can purposefully achieve something. It is a cognitive training meant to preserve and perhaps somewhat improve their capabilities. Marijke Magermann is a speech therapist and, in addition, full of ideas of how to create fun activities for the patients.

In the afternoon Marijke Magermann, within the setting of the animation group, offers entertainment where the patients are encouraged to participate actively . Marijke is sparkling with energy and 'joie de vivre' and tries to carry the patients with her; she has brought music and a big red microphone. She plays well-known melodies, handing the microphone around and inviting one patient after another to join in the singing. There are songs and hits of various styles and from different periods of time, so that for everyone there might be something that they know and which encourages them to join in. Some patients don't want to. Others take the microphone, but then remain silent or grumble something to themselves. It does not matter because it is covered by the music coming from the tape recorder. Marijke's cheerfulness is catching, the moods are livening up and after a while one patient after another really joins in and is enthusiastically applauded.

The young man I had noticed that morning at the coffee break is here too. He still seems shy and apathetic. A nurse sitting next to him tries several times to encourage him to take the microphone, but he does not want to. Yet, I see that as soon as nobody is paying attention to him, he is humming and obviously enjoys swaying his body with the rhythm of the music. This swaying is quite different from his earlier stereotyped rocking, and once he is even laughing. But as soon as somebody is addressing him, he withdraws and falls back into mechanical rocking. Once more, it is amazing to observe how, if we are perceptive of nuances, the same behaviour — in this case the swaying of the body — with the same person can express totally different things. Again the 'how' is much more important than the 'what'; this knowledge, together with the sensitivity for nuances, should be increasingly emphasised in both training and further education of people working in this field.

Spirits rise higher and higher. It seems to me that Marijke sometimes is a little bit too active, but quite obviously she is really present with her heart and has the gift to get the patients out of their lethargy. They visibly enjoy themselves. After all the tapes have been played, Marijke asks if somebody knows another song. One of the men sings a folk song, another a sailor's song, and when one of the men starts singing the national anthem, some others get up and stand to attention.

All at once an elderly patient, who up to now had been silent, takes the microphone and sings: 'Je suis seul ce soir' ('I am alone tonight'), the whole song from beginning to end. Everybody is listening spellbound. It is a moving moment that makes us feel intensely the loneliness and longing from which probably not only the singer, but also every patient here, is suffering.

Then coffee is served. At first there are not enough cups and among the patients a little scramble is going on to get one. One of the patients energetically pushes a cup in front of me, though he is otherwise trying to get as many as possible for himself and even drinks from his neighbours' cups when they are not paying attention.

Marijke Magerman thinks that the group is too big, yet more and more patients want to join, and she does not want to turn anybody down. Again, some nurses are joyfully participating. Co-operation seems to work well within the context of this programme. Of course, these activities have nothing directly to do with Pre-Therapy, yet something of the fundamental idea comes through: to meet patients with acceptance, believe them capable of doing things, take them seriously and accept them as they are. This was also Garry Prouty's impression at his last visit in Beernem as shown by his statement in the video tape recorded at the occasion.

3. St Jan-Berchmans — a ward undergoing radical change

The new concept of St Jan-Berchmans had been initiated by a governmental decree requiring that by July 1, 1995, a new ward had to be opened for patients whose condition was so stabilised that they no longer needed explicit psychiatric treatment. This new ward was to be more of a nursing home and give the patients more rights and freedom. This was not so much decided for humanitarian as for economic reasons, because nursing wards can charge higher rates. Yet at the same time it was a chance for developing new concepts that would better fit the patients' needs.

Two years went by without any preparations for the forthcoming changes. Only very shortly before the set day was it decided that St Jan-Berchmans, the most ancient ward at Sint-Amandus, should temporarily be converted into a nursing ward. In a few years the whole ward will be transferred to Bruges, where the residents will have more conveniences and opportunities for leisure activities so then the higher rates will be justified. But for the time being, patients as well as nurses have to make do with the inconveniences of this interim solution and come to terms with the problems it poses.

The start was considerably inhibited by the lack of preparation and adequate information. Not one day earlier than July 1, 1995, the new ward opened and work at St Jan-Berchmans began. The patients were informed at the last moment that they were to be transferred. Many of them could not understand why they had to go to St Jan-Berchmans. For example there were patients, who before had a single room and now had to share a room with up to three room mates. To them it meant a decline instead of an improvement. In addition, there was the bad reputation attached to this ward. Up to now, to be sent to St Jan-Berchmans had been considered a punishment for a patient. This made it hard to adopt a positive attitude. Some patients were ashamed of having to move there, although it was a rehabilitation project. The staff had wished that at least the name of the ward could have changed, but to no avail.

Chris Van Wyngene takes me to St Jan-Berchmans. It is a dark old brick building looking quite forbidding from the outside. But inside a freer atmosphere is immediately sensed, even if the appearance at first sight does not differ much from other wards. Here too, some men are sitting around in the living room, dozing apathetically, looking at the newspaper, not showing much of a reaction. But somehow the mood is more relaxed: there is less tension in the air than in the other wards I have seen.

'At first we were suspicious about this new way of working, because it was mainly introduced for economic reasons, not for the well-being of the patients,' explains *Ralf Bonte* who is showing me the ward. 'But now, after eighteen months, I can say that it is much more rewarding to work in this way. We try to manifest the principles dictated by the government in a way the patients can benefit from.

It is a paradox though, that the patients here have to pay more than on a ward where psychiatric treatment is provided, but that at the same time we have less staff. For thirty patients the government provides twelve positions, but this number includes everything — administration, sports, workshops, etc. The fact is that we have six nurses for thirty patients, plus a night watch. This means there are two working on the morning shift from 6 a.m. to 2.30 p.m., but in the afternoon shift and on weekends we work alone. Yet, particularly in the evenings and on weekends so many social activities are possible that cannot be managed by just one person. It is very difficult for us to organise the things we would like to.'

Ralf Bonte, like Koen Vanquathem whom I had met the day before, works on the ward as a psychological assistant. Their task is to put into practice the new project while at the same time working as full-time nurses. They have mixed feelings about new changes they have to cope with because the ward has recently been split up into three parts. This has the advantage that the groups are smaller, but at the same time is problematic because the patients were split up just by administrative measures, without taking into account their own wishes or suggestions from the staff. Through this splitting, each group is thrown back on its own resources. The mutual exchange and support the staff was aiming at gets more difficult. They are still trying out things and searching for the best way to work. They have learned a lot, but suffered setbacks as well.

'A person who comes here after having lived for such a long time on a closed ward needs time to get accustomed. I hope that within two or three years many patients will know more clearly what they really want,' says Chris Van Wyngene, who follows the project as a consultant and does individual therapy with some of the patients.

People, who for years just have done what they were told, sometimes cannot cope with the new freedom. Making decisions for themselves even if it is only which clothes they want to wear, is extremely difficult for them. It needs time for the patients to get used to, and learning to make use of, more freedom. They need structures that help them with it.

Once more, an example concerning personal hygiene may illustrate it: 'At the beginning it was completely free,' Ralf reports, 'we just told them that they had to wash every day. But we had to back-track, because some of the patients didn't wash themselves at all. We had to introduce the rule of a bath twice a week. And we have to pay attention to their washing and shaving every morning. Because it impairs their whole well-being, if they neglect themselves too much. So we ask that they take a bath or a shower twice a week, one between Monday morning and Tuesday evening, the other between Thursday morning and Friday evening, they can choose when they want to do it. They can decide, for example, today I don't feel so well, I prefer to take my shower in the evening instead in the morning as usual.'

This is a good example of a structure that is helpful because it makes the necessary minimum demands, but at the same time offers some free choice. One of the basic principles of person-centred work, 'as little structure as possible and as much as necessary', is true for every area. Yet it requires of the carers sensitively to recognise the structure which might be helpful for a patient and which will restrict him, the choices which are enabling and which are stressing him. Carers must be able to understand accurately the reactions of their clients and be flexible in their ways of responding. This balance cannot not be established by routine and then fixed for ever, but must be constantly rediscovered and remade. Moreover it needs patience to allow this balance to settle down. Often much too quickly it is concluded that it does not work.

Koen Vanquaethem has experienced it: 'Unfortunately the closets are locked here, and the patients cannot by themselves get to their belongings. We had asked that the closets were left open. They were left unlocked, but after a week it was a big mess, and therefore they got locked again. For twenty years the patients have been used to that. It cannot be changed within two weeks, but would have needed a longer attempt.'

'It is a new way of thinking which not everybody is yet ready for,' says Ralf Bonte. He gives some examples of how the new approach is working in practice: 'For example, before, if a patient had to go to the hospital, he was taken there by a taxi service and had to work out for himself how to cope with this new and threatening situation. Instead now I take him to the hospital, see him to his room, help him to unpack his things, express my understanding for his anxiety and nervousness, understanding that I would be nervous and anxious myself if I had to go to a hospital for an operation. It was not easy to convince the administration that this change was necessary. But I could prove that doing it this way we would even save money. They see everything just from an administrative and financial viewpoint. They have no contact with the patients. For example, there is this rule that when we go somewhere, we always have to take as many patients as possible with us. But there are situations when it is very important to go with a patient alone; for instance to buy clothes. Or, once I went with a patient to the beach, because he had so much wanted to do that. There has to be space sometimes for such individual concerns.

On the other hand, it is very important for us to improve their ways of living together in the group, to foster consideration for each other, for example when having coffee, to take care that everybody gets some. A patient who is much weaker than the others is 'mothered' by the stronger patients. We would not like him to be transferred to another group. He is important for the others and they have a good influence on him. They make exceptions for him if necessary, help him at meals, and care for him.'

Congruence is essential for Ralf Bonte — once in a while to say something about himself too, being transparent as a person not only in his function as a 'nurse'. At the beginning, Ralf had also tried to sit with the patients and work with contact reflections, but he could not come to terms with it. 'I was the only one in our team to do that. Didn't get any support. Somehow it was just not possible. But what I took from Prouty was the attitude.'

I agree that the attitude is the most essential aspect, but explain to him how important reflections are for facilitating the patients' contact with their experiencing. Chris van Wyngene shares my opinion: 'Verbalising something helps the patients becoming aware of it. It is important for them to realise what is happening to them.' Long-term stays on closed wards further reduce the patients' perceptual awareness which is already impaired by their illness. They often can bear the situation only by sealing themselves off.

Ralf Bonte sees us through the house. He points with regret to the obsolete sanitary facilities we have to cross to get to a quiet back room, where the patients can withdraw. A man who used to work for an architect is sitting on a table drawing a plan for a house. There is also an old computer at the patients' disposal that had been bought second hand.

The tables in the living room, where the patients also take their meals, are covered with green tablecloths. On the wall there is a schedule that shows who is working this week and when they will be on duty, so that the residents always know when their personal carer will be there. On this ward, each patient has his personal carer who he can turn to with his questions and concerns. The menu too is hanging on the wall, and the actual day and month. These notices help the residents with their orientation and support their reality contact. Also each group has two television sets, so that there is a choice and not everybody has to watch the same programme.

There is a small workshop where spices are packed for a woman selling them on the market. It is a small private commission that gives the men something to do, if they want to. Ralf shows us the garden: he is happy that the door is no longer locked and the fence has been removed so that everybody can easily get in and out.

We look at the bedrooms upstairs. In one department the rooms have four beds. Though they are quite spacious, they look more like sheds than rooms, as they are separated from each other by walls, but open to the corridor and have no doors. At the end of the corridor there is a room with a number of sinks — they had had to fight for those, Ralf says; before, there had been no washing facilities upstairs. The next department is the most comfortable. It offers quite cosy one- and two-bedded rooms, two of them even are furnished with the residents' own furniture.

The small room for the night staff can be used by the patients during the day. At my visit, a man is sitting there at a table, typing on an old typewriter — writing poems, he explains. We exchange a few words about writing poems.

There are many little points on this ward where the individuality of the patients is taken more into consideration. And these little things are what — despite the unfavourable circumstances — make up the freer atmosphere that I noticed when first entering this house.

Conclusion

Despite some difficulties, the project group by now is well anchored at Sint-Amandus. The team had been invited by government psychiatrists and inspectors to give a presentation of their project, which had been well received. 'It is not as difficult any more as it had been at the beginning,' the therapists admit. 'It depends very much on training standards, there are increasingly younger people whose professional education conforms more with what we are aiming at.' Some time ago, Bea Coninckx was asked for help by a ward that up to then had refused to have anything to do with the project; now she works there with a patient. The project group feels affirmed also by the fact that all the psychiatrists of the hospital are referring patients to them. And the new thinking at St Jan-Berchmans too is reinforcing them in their approach that is starting to spread further.

What has changed for the initiator of the Pre-Therapy project since he started it? Dr Luc Roelens has no opportunity to work explicitly with Pre-Therapy. With the large number of patients he has to care for there is no time for it. Nevertheless, his way of working is influenced by Pre-Therapy: 'Being patient, waiting, asking very small questions, not pushing the patients, approaching them in small steps. I learned from Prouty to work in the client's tempo. Or, if this is not possible, at least to keep in mind that it is important and perhaps give the nurses a hint.' Co-operation with the nursing staff is very important to him. 'We can mutually influence each other. Therapists too have to communicate with the nurses, and a patient should find understanding for what he is preoccupied with not only in therapy, but also in daily life.'

Luc Roelens is working in a very client-centred way, yet he emphasises that sometimes it is necessary to be strict and set clear limits for the patients: 'We cannot tolerate, for example, that somebody is drinking five to six litres of water a day and then incessantly has to go to the toilet. We can understand that this is important for him, that it is his way to feel alive, we must try to talk with him about it, but nevertheless, we have to stop it.' This too is a question of balance between structure and freedom that is so essential in person-centred work. Understanding and accepting does not mean a 'laissez faire' approach.

Dr Roelens still has the overall responsibility for the project. But the project group now works to a great extent autonomously. He sees what they have achieved and thinks that it would be time to evaluate it in a research project. 'We begin to see changes in the chronic patients. The project today is a stable value at Sint-Amandus,' he states with satisfaction.

The project group knows this too: 'We are there, we cannot be ignored any more.'

After I got home, I got a letter from Beernem — the patient with whom I had had a short conversation at St Jan-Berchmans had asked for my address and sent me one of his poems. I shall conclude my report with it:

Introspection

When you leave
the booming city's heart

and descend
into the somber caverns

of death

You still see far before you
the half-shadow

of a young widow
growing minor flowers

and blowing before her the down
of overblown dandelions

While black sheep
run out of her hand, unbridled

In the somber caverns of death
her near-shadow

will shine intensely coloured

a rainbow intense
to your scarce sun opposed

Piet Labian

Chapter 2

Further Evolutions of
Pre-Therapy

Progress into Europe

Coming to Europe was an important step for Garry Prouty as well as for the evolution of Pre-Therapy. His first workshop outside the USA took place in 1985 in Breda, Holland. It was the beginning of Pre-Therapy in Europe. Not only did it offer the first opportunity to meet Garry Prouty and his work in a European country, it consequently resulted in its participants making substantial contributions to the further development of Pre-Therapy (among others Dion Van Werde, Luc Roelens and Hans Peters, who have become major representatives). For Prouty this workshop provided the acknowledgment he needed to continue his work.

Since then he has visited Europe regularly, has presented his approach at numerous international conferences and has held seminars in many countries (Belgium, the Czech Republic, Germany, Greece, Italy, the Netherlands, Romania, Slovakia and the UK). Many of the participants in these seminars — psychologists, psychiatrists, nurses and other professionals — consequently apply Pre-Therapy, to a greater or lesser extent, in different professional areas and under various conditions. Through practice, training and research they contribute to the further evolution and spread of Pre-Therapy. I have had extensive conversations with some of them when preparing this book — their views will appear in the following chapters.

Apart from the first beginnings in the USA, it was in Europe that Pre-Therapy found the necessary acceptance and support for its development and spread. This in turn had an influence back in the USA where Prouty's work has become increasingly acknowledged and valued in recent years. Unfortunately though, some projects became victims of the tendency to privatise health systems. A three-year research programme in co operation with the Osteopathic Hospital in Chicago has been dropped at short notice after the hospital was sold to a financial corporation.

In Europe too, such tendencies increasingly threaten to become the norm. Therefore it is increasingly important that here, for many years, successful programmes exist that can no longer be overlooked. Besides the two long-term projects in Belgium described in Part 2 and chapter one of Part 3, in every country where Prouty did workshops, there are therapists, nurses and carers who have picked up and transferred the approach in various ways into their practice, some on a quite regular base, others just occasionally. Yet, every attempt to integrate Pre-Therapy represents a contribution to its further development and propagation.

In 1995 the *Pre-Therapy International Network* was founded in Amsterdam, in order to facilitate exchanges and co-operation between the countries and professionals who work with Pre-Therapy. The Network is located in Gent, Belgium[1], and aims to develop and offer training programmes as well as to facilitate the co-ordination of training initiatives in many countries. A quarterly newsletter is published and a yearly meeting organised for its members.

Pre-Therapeutic approaches in different professional fields

1. In psychiatric hospitals
Even if there is no officially-introduced Pre-Therapy programme in a hospital, individual professionals who have participated in a Prouty workshop do apply it in different ways, whether it is officially introduced or arrives through common knowledge. Often Pre-Therapeutic elements are included in their day-to-day tasks or individual Pre-Therapy sessions with certain patients.

Dr Wim Lucieer (interview December 1, 1996 in Breda, Holland), another participant on Prouty's first European workshop, worked for many years as a clinical psychiatrist in a psychiatric hospital. Today, besides being a psychotherapist in private practice, he teaches at a clinical training institute and works as a psychiatric consultant for different organisations.

He used to integrate pre-therapeutic approaches into his work as a psychiatrist on a ward for acute patients and found this particularly helpful in crisis situations, such as emergency admissions. He explains, 'In these situations it is important to build up trust and understanding with the patient, so that we can talk about the necessary measures to take, for example medication. It makes much more sense to give a patient an injection to which he agrees, than to do it against his will.' He has used Pre-Therapy not only in emergency admissions, but also in many other difficult situations.

'PETER is a chronic schizophrenic patient who has lived at the clinic for many years, psychosis had raged in him for a very long time and made him an apathetic and withdrawn person. For as long as I have known him, he was mostly in his room listening to music, not doing anything else. Yet I was told that in former years, before my time, he used to play chess and to go out to concerts and so on. But now, this was all gone and he was very

---

1. Contact address: Dion Van Werde, Neuro-Psychiatrische Kliniek Sint-Camillus, Beukenlaan 20, B-9051, Sint-Denijs-Westreem, Belgium.

restricted indeed by the effects of schizophrenia and long-term psychiatric hospitalisation. From time to time he suffered from very frightening, very bizarre hallucinatory attacks. I was informed about these by the nurses, who thought that he did not tolerate the medication. They said he was confused and complaining about feeling dizzy. I asked them to call me the next time it happened. I wanted to see him, before prescribing new medication. One day they called me.

W   **Hello Peter, the head nurse called me. I hear that you are not feeling well.**
                    [No movement, no answer . . . After a while . . .]
W   **Peter, I am Wim, I came to see you, because I was told that you are not well. Is it OK for you that I am here?'**
                    [He made a tiny movement with his head from which I concluded that it was OK . . . After a while . . .]
W   **I see anxiety in your face, and I think that you are suffering.**

Here I see a difference from what Garry is doing; my patients are not as regressed as those Garry describes. We have to meet the clients on the level where they are. With some whom I know well and who know me well, I don't work just strictly with reflections, but apply the principle in a somewhat extended way. I have discussed this case with Garry and he shared my opinion.

W   **I am Wim, Peter. I have the impression that you are very frightened. I hope I will be able to help you.**
                    [After a while . . .]
W   **I see your eyes moving.**
                    [. . . A moment later.]
W   **Are you looking for something, Peter, are you looking for something?'**
                    [. . . After a while . . .]
W   **Your eyes look to the ceiling. It looks as if you were frightened, Peter. Do you see something?**
                    [And again after a while . . .]
W   **Perhaps you want to tell me something about it?**

This again is something more than what Garry would do, but I sensed that there was some kind of contact, though he did not say anything, therefore I felt free to respond this way.

          [And then – he still did not move and nothing had changed, but nevertheless I felt that I could read something like irritation in his face . . .]

W	It seemed to me that you were irritated. Are you angry with me for talking with you?' *[And again there was a tiny movement in his face. He seemed wanting to tell me that it did not make him angry and that he did not want me to go away . . . So after a while . . .]*
W	I am here with you Peter, in this room. This is your room.
W	The nurse called me. He is concerned about you. He thinks that you are suffering. *[. . . And it continued this way for a while, and then something changed. All at once . . .]*
P	Tree.
W	Tree. *[And after a while . . .]* Tree, I think you said tree, Peter. *[No reaction . . . After a while . . .]* I am sitting here with you, Peter, in your room. And I heard you say, 'Tree'. And I see your eyes looking at the ceiling. Do you see a tree there? *[And all of a sudden, without any change in his catatonic state . . .]*
P	A plastic tree.
W	A plastic tree. *[And after a very long silence during which I had the impression that his tension was diminishing and contact increasing, he suddenly said in a very frightened voice . . .]*
P	I am a little leaf. I am falling.
W	You tell me that you see a plastic tree and that you are a little leaf that is falling. And I can see it in your face that this is a very frightening experience. I can imagine how frightening it is.' *[That's how I do it. It is an invitation somehow, a participation. And all at once the catatonia was gone. He took my hands . . .]*
P	I am glad you are here. *[He was silent for a while . . .]* And now we are both frightened.
W	No, Peter, I am Wim. You are Peter. We are here in this room, in your room. I see your record player, I see your records, we talk about very difficult things. I can see your fear and can feel how frightened you are. I am not frightened. It is your fear.

This is what Gendlin calls the specification of feelings.

'Well, this was Peter a few years ago. He is still suffering from schizophrenia and now lives on a ward for chronic patients. But his condition has considerably improved. The day I could free him from an acute schizophrenic episode was an important day. A lot of trust has built up then, so that later I could try a new medication, a medication that was not without danger but extremely effective for chronic schizophrenia. I proposed to treat him with this medication and explained him what its effects were and also told him about the dangers. I think that, because of the experience we had had together, he trusted me and agreed. He was one of the first patients to take this medication. And it obviously helped him. He now plays chess again, goes to concerts and participates in quite a number of other activities.'

This is one of many convincing examples Wim Lucieer has shared with me. They show how useful and necessary Pre-Therapy can be for a psychiatrist working in a psychiatric hospital.

'The problem with doctors of exclusively medical orientation is that they just look at symptoms and only treat those. They do not see the other side, for which there is no medical solution. Of course, I look at the symptoms too, but then I forget about them and look at the inner side. That's where the resources are. If I do accept a patient in his suffering and not just reduce him to his symptoms, I also appeal to these resources, and that is how acceptance may provoke change.

The important thing is, that in such moments we have to be well anchored ourselves, that we are not afraid. The client must sense that the therapist feels OK — at least in this moment — that he is not scared, not nervous, that he is there for the patient, open and ready for whatever will come. Gendlin has underlined, how important that is when dealing with psychosis and in psychiatry in general. And something else to me is very important — I don't know if this is Pre-Therapy or Client-Centred Therapy — I always say things in a way that makes it very easy for the patient to reply: 'No, that's not the way it is.' It is important to establish contact and not just to give medication without asking. We have to give ourselves a little time to ask and to explain why we want to give this medication. Even when people refuse medication, I respond to that too, it is very important. Trust is essential when giving medication.'

Wim Lucieer was working for several years as a psychiatrist in Dar-es-Salaam and teaching at the university there. His African experiences had a crucial influence on his basic attitude.

'Contact is essential when working in another culture. Contact without words. Just being there. That helped me. At the beginning I only knew a little Kishuaheli. So I looked for non verbal hints. And I tried to figure out what they were talking about and what they might say and later on I checked it out. This way I learned to carefully pay attention to the non-verbal.' Later, it was not a big step for Wim Lucieer to adopt the principles of Pre-Therapy. And he sees another parallel: 'Laughing — not laughing *about* but laughing *with* people. Garry too makes this difference. In Africa they laugh with a crazy person, and all at once she is laughing too. This too is a way of establishing contact — with her crazy world.

'Since I have been in Africa, and today when working with refugees, I increasingly think about the cultural roots of psychiatry and psychotherapy. Medicine and psychiatry (and in a sense also psychoanalysis) are rooted in a reductionistic natural science. Whereas Rogers embodies the 'American Dream', the ideal of wholeness and congruence of human beings. Individual freedom (in community with others) remains an ideal worth striving for. However, Garry's work responds to the suffering of our century: homelessness with all its social and psychological consequences. Anchoring is the key word.'

Dr Lucieer has always tried to involve the nurses and to raise their understanding for the patients' behaviours. He explained to them that what the patients express is not just nonsense, and encouraged them to sit at their bedside once in a while and try to make contact. Prouty had been invited several times to the hospital, so some of the nurses already knew about Pre-Therapy and were open to Wim Lucieer's suggestions.

Dr Aldo Dinacci, on different occasions, worked individually with Pre-Therapy within the institutional setting of a psychiatric hospital. He is a psychologist in Bologna. Some years ago, at the Presidio Psichiatrico St Niccolo in Siena, he had the opportunity to do Pre-Therapy with patients, in the context of a research project (Dinacci 1994, 1995). He worked with some chronic patients diagnosed as schizophrenic — a diagnosis that nearly all patients there were labelled with, as Dinacci sarcastically states. These patients were at the hospital for years or even decades. They live there, forgotten by their relatives, under precarious conditions and very poorly cared for. Even for medical care, dentistry etc., there is only money in case of extreme emergency.

Aldo Dinacci developed scales allowing him to measure quantitative and qualitative changes in contact behaviour during the therapy sessions. He did a comparative study with four patients, two of them having an equal number of Pre-Therapy sessions over a period of six months. One was 45, and at the hospital for 30 years, the other 67 and at the hospital for 55 years, and both were considered schizophrenic and having severe mental disabilities. Two other patients offering similar conditions were used as a control group and had just one interview at the beginning and one at the end of the six months. After this period, there was evidence of remarkable changes with those patients who had had Pre-Therapy, whereas the condition of the other two remained unchanged.

Dinacci has documented his work on video tapes that demonstrate how, with the help of Pre-Therapy, he makes contact with these 'forgotten' patients who for years were living a miserable existence, completely isolated within themselves, and who now begin slowly to communicate. I saw these videos several times and remember strongly an old, nearly toothless man who at the beginning just utters grumbling sounds, whereas in a later sequence he says — with some difficulty but still — in clearly understandable words: 'It is not good here. At home it was good.' And the old man who has lived at this hospital for decades repeats these words over and over again.

Yet, after a while, Dinacci's work at the hospital was no longer welcomed for fear that it might stir up trouble; he was forced to leave. Later — besides having his own practice — he worked with some patients in another psychiatric hospital in Imola, Italy. After promising beginnings (also documented by videos), the situation there seemed to become difficult too.

2. In psychotherapeutic practice
Bart Santen (interview December 1, 1996 in Breda) works as a psychotherapist in a psychiatric hospital for children and adolescents and in private practice in Breda. He is credited with organising Prouty's first European workshop in Breda, in 1985. What impact did meeting Prouty and Pre-Therapy have on his work?
> 'We should never imitate Garry. Everybody has to find his or her own way. What I see with Prouty is that however the person is moving, whatever is going on in her, he will pick up something, perceive something. This is a consistent factor that is very important in my own work too.'

Bart Santen, in his practice, has often to work with multiple personalities and finds that with them the concept of Pre-Therapy is particularly helpful.
> 'All these parts that have become autonomous, in whatever role they might appear, it is always this person. Multiple personalities have quite strong reactions when I estimate or accept one of these parts more than others, when I am afraid of certain parts or reinforcing some parts more than others. The clients will accurately and sensitively perceive it — and therefore show no more of themselves than a façade. This makes it impossible to really meet each other. It is very important to be open for all the parts in a client, to approach them all without fear — also those that are terrorising by intrapsychically repeating earlier experiences — and to make contact with all of them. That does not mean that we don't have to fight some tendencies. We should not allow one tendency to actively reject and try to terrorise other tendencies. I accept the reality, necessity and history of its existence, but I do not allow it to just act out. We have to show solidarity with every part, but never at the expense of other parts. We have to find ways to meet them all. And it has to be perceptible for the client that we dare to do that, that we are not afraid. It helps the client imagining that perhaps one day she might herself overcome her fear. And I think when we are able to take over this burden we have Pre-Therapy.
> 'I think that Garry, in his total commitment, is not afraid. He will certainly never run any risks with his clients, but he is not afraid when something heavy is coming up, he is just there. And this is essential for a client, to experience that the therapist is not afraid. Of course, therapists have fears, I have too, but we have to come to terms with them, to work on them in order to preserve the integrity of our presence and of our goals.'

Presence, for Bart Santen, does not mean, 'imposing closeness. To be there may also mean respecting distance.' He sees psychotherapy as a skill, and to him it is important 'To be a good therapist also in terms of methods, to be aware of what is necessary and what is going on. But it does not work when I am not really there as a person.' What to him is exemplary with Garry Prouty is 'the right form of commitment, patience, openness for many facets, not moralising and above all his presence.'

Dr Ton Coffeng (interview November 29, 1996 in Amsterdam) is a psychiatrist and psychotherapist at a therapy centre in Friesland (Holland). Moreover, he is a trainer and supervisor for client-centred psychotherapists as well as being involved in training for psychiatrists and nurses. He first met Prouty in 1981 and was impressed by his approach which he saw as a more humane alternative to psychiatry. He participated in workshops with Garry Prouty and studied his writings. Then he started to integrate Pre-Therapy into his continuing training programmes for psychiatric nurses and to present Prouty's approach in several psychiatric hospitals in Holland. In 1994 he organised a workshop with Garry Prouty in Amsterdam.

'I was fascinated by Prouty, though I do not work with chronic schizophrenic or mentally handicapped people,' says Dr Coffeng, who has specialised in treating trauma patients (Coffeng, 1994, 1995, 1996, 1997). In his experience, for them, the usual therapeutic approaches are not sufficient and focusing does not really work. Prouty's Pre-Therapy and his concept of pre-symbolic experiencing proved to be a better approach. Ton Coffeng mentions an example: 'I have a video with a confused patient where I just sit on the floor with her, doing nothing else than word by word reflections. And all at once she asks: "May I draw it?" And she does a very childlike drawing of her confused state of mind.'

Like Bart Santen, Ton Coffeng emphasises the importance with multiple personalities of 'accepting every part, because it helps the client to integrate it.' He does not believe in more directive methods, 'Where the therapist talks first with one side and then with the other and then asks for a choice. We have to take seriously all the parts because for the person they are real, and therefore it is best to just reflect what we perceive.' For Ton Coffeng this is not a matter of technique, 'We must understand what this attitude means.' It is very important to him that 'the client is the "expert"'. He works with reflections, yet above all, in a larger sense with an attitude that takes the patient seriously the way he is.

Ton Coffeng too worked for some time in Africa. And like Wim Lucieer, he feels that this experience sharpened his sensitivity for Pre-Therapy: 'In Africa repeating is a common way of conversation,' he explains. 'It seems to be a basic way of communicating that we have lost.'

Ute Binder expresses similar ideas (interview March 16, 1997, Frankfurt a. Main) when she declares that repeating is a way of communicating in early childhood. Mothers communicate this way with small children, thus quite naturally helping them to develop their contact functions. Prouty's contact reflections therefore might also help people to catch up with missed stages of development.

Ute Binder works as a psychotherapist in private practice in Frankfurt a. Main. She predominantly sees ambulant psychotic patients and works consistently in a client-centred way. For her, empathy is the essential element of psychotherapy (Binder, 1994a, 1994b, 1996). She is integrating Pre-Therapy in a perfectly smooth transition into Client-Centred Psychotherapy, thus very naturally following the clients on their contact level according to what Van Werde calls the grey-zone functioning.

Her patients, for the most part, are not in such a regressive state that pure contact reflections would be indicated. So she has developed a method she calls 'doubling', where she combines pre-therapeutic contact reflections with the usual client-centred reflecting of feelings. She says for example: 'Your eyes are wet' (facial reflection) immediately adding: 'You are sad' (verbalisation of feelings). Doubling addresses the patient on two levels at the same time: on the one hand making contact, on the other stimulating self-exploration. Both are equally important.

For her too, the fundamental significance of Prouty's concepts goes far beyond contact reflections. She considers reality contact an essential aspect of her work. What therapist and client both can perceive, ' "the common third" in the sense of Wolfgang Pfeiffer — "das gemeinsame Dritte" (Pfeiffer, 1993) — offers a point of reference and allows meeting each other without feeling threatened by too close a relation.'

For Ute Binder it is necessary to 'establish something that makes patients realise that they are in control of the situation, makes them feel that I can bring something about and it works. I can trust that. I can reliably bring something about. Reliability is important, without it the effect would be negative. The opposite experience leads to emotional collapse.'

On the emotional level too, it is important to pick up that which both are aware of. Shared feelings foster emotional contact and verbalising them helps the client to differentiate, 'Where are we alike, where are we different?' For example a patient can be silent when it gets too threatening, and tension builds up. Ute Binder reflects this tension that they both sense: 'There it is again, isn't it?' This way the patient can feel that other people are not that different from her. 'We both feel it, we can solve it by talking about it', is what Ute Binder wants to communicate.

Helmuth Beutel (interview May 2, 1997, Esslingen, Germany) is a psychotherapist in private practice in Esslingen near Stuttgart. He too works with psychotic outpatients and uses Pre-Therapy particularly for crisis interventions. When clients are going through a psychotic episode, he tries to establish their contact with the surrounding reality and with themselves by situational and body reflections, so that they might come back to solid ground.

'A patient, 17 years old, fell ill with paranoid schizophrenia. The prognosis was not favourable, he was hospitalised six times and treated, among other, with electro-shocks. He believed that other people could read his thoughts, had paranoid fears and was persuaded of the apocalypse being imminent. During the therapy sessions, these ideas were barely talked about, but I tried with body reflections and situational reflections to help him finding a new relation with himself and with the reality of the actual situation, here in this room. The interpersonal aspect was important too. I told him what I perceived in my reality. This helped him letting go of the threatening ideas and perceiving what was around him, thus getting to a more relaxed and more adequate reality perception. He now lives at home and is working half-day. He gets medication and comes to psychotherapy regularly.

'This way it is often possible to minimise a psychotic episode, so that there is no need for hospitalising the patient and he can continue his outpatient psychotherapy.'

3. In organisations for people with special needs
Dr Hans Peters (interview November 1996, Nijmegen, Holland), now retired, has a doctorate in special education and at the time of the interview worked in a community for people with special needs in Ottersum which had 700 residents living there, partly in small units. Hans Peters originally was a behaviour therapist and, in addition, has a training in Client-Centred Psychotherapy. In his opinion, both approaches can be easily combined and complement each other (Peters, 1984, 1992a, 2001).

'For understanding disabled persons, the attitude they are met with is essential, therefore we need the Client-Centred Approach. But we also need to act,' says Hans Peters, 'The Client-Centred Approach neglects action, whereas in behaviour therapy accurate listening is neglected. Yet, before being able to act, we need to understand.' Here Prouty's concept offers a bridge. Hans Peters sees Pre-Therapy as a part of Client-Centred Psycho-therapy, but for him, 'Prouty is the only one in the client-centred field who is consciously using action. Pre-Therapy is an act of understanding that implements action.'

He emphasises the importance of the right distance. 'Some clients are afraid of contact. Then we have to find a distant contact. This is empathy.' Here Peters clearly differentiates himself from a common misunderstanding (also to be found in the person-centred field) that equates empathy with closeness. This contradicts the client-centred principle of always entering the clients' frame of reference that includes recognising and respecting their need for distance.

Dr Peters is responsible for the psychotherapeutic services offered to the residents of this organisation. He is supported by four assistants, and to one of them he has introduced Pre-Therapy. Peters does therapy 'on the spot' where the clients are in the moment. He goes to see them when the situation asks for it. 'Not regularly. I go to see them when there are questions or problems.'

There is a revealing video tape showing two sequences with a severely disabled and very aggressive women. In the first sequence, we see her with a carer who, in a critical situation, tries to persuade and calm her down. Though this is done in a very gentle and caring way, it provokes the client to get even more violently aggressive till, finally exhausted, she pulls the blanket over her head. It is clearly visible how she is rejecting to be touched, obviously at that moment experiencing it as offending. The second sequence shows Hans Peters with the same client working with pre-therapeutic reflections, especially body reflections. The client is increasingly relaxed, and a gentle, almost humorous, mostly non-verbal contact develops between him and her. The video tape was recorded about three years before the interview. Hans Peters states, that the client never since had such aggressive episodes.

For Hans Peters, equally important as psychotherapy, is the way carers deal with the residents and their problems in daily life (Peters 1992b). Part of his work therefore consists in consulting and training the staff. He has introduced Pre-Therapy to the institution, and now several wards work with it. The staff are quite open for this way of working because they experience it also as a relief for themselves. For example, there was a client who before, by repeating the same remarks and questions over and over again, had constantly provoked stressful and energy-consuming fights; with the help of contact reflections this behaviour could considerably be reduced.

'Reflecting helps developing a person-centred attitude, making contact in daily life and understanding the disabled persons better. Particularly very aggressive or verbally aggressive, destructive clients can be approached through contact reflections in a way they understand and that is reassuring them. Reflections prevent escalation. There is considerably less fighting', says Hans Peters. 'Pre-Therapy is not only a very effective form of therapy (for instance in treatment of psychosis and depression), but also an attitude, a way to communicate with difficult clients. Reflections help to calm and slow them down, especially but not only, psychotic people. Pre-Therapy is particularly indicated for persons with severe disabilities. With mildly disabled people reflecting sometimes might be too confrontational.'

For Hans Peters the most significant long-term effect of working with Pre-Therapy is, 'Less tension for the staff. To work this way is obviously reducing stress. The staff knows how to respond to aggressive people. This is a very important base.'

At the Diakonie Stetten, a big organisation for people with special needs near Stuttgart, Germany, several psychologists are beginning to integrate Pre-Therapy into their work that includes doing therapy with the residents and consulting the staff. Some have participated in seminars with Garry Prouty. In addition, in 1995/96, I was invited to do a series of supervision sessions with the whole team of psychologists working at the Diakonie Stetten. Two of them, *Michael Kief* and *Hermann Kolbe*, describe in two examples their experiences with Pre-Therapy (interview March 1997, Stetten).

Michael Kief worked for about two years (60 to 70 sessions) with a woman living in a women's group where she showed severely disturbed behaviours (states of excitement, aggressive eruptions). She frequently had to be separated from the others and locked up in her room. Initially, during the sessions she just uttered her typical incoherent and nearly unintelligible words stereotypically providing them all with the same invented endings. With the help of reflections, the therapist gradually succeeded in making contact, and simple realistic questions and answers became possible. The stereotypical expressions and suffixes diminished and the vocabulary expanded. The client obviously could make use of the therapeutic setting. She now lives in a mixed group, where she has much more freedom. Only very rarely is it necessary to lock her in her room, as the attacks on her fellow patients have nearly stopped. Instructed by the therapist, now the staff also works with pre-therapeutic contact reflections.

Hermann Kolbe worked for two months with a severely disabled woman who has only a rudimentary vocabulary and expresses herself only through fragments of words or phrases. She is able to eat, drink and dress herself. Her attitude towards the staff was predominantly reluctant, mistrusting and not honest. Her face looks petrified; very rarely does she show an emotion. She is greedy to excess, stuffs into her mouth whatever she can find, steals from the plates of the other residents, and is excessively gaining weight. For some time the staff tried to strictly control her eating habits; now the tendency is more to leave her alone.

Hermann Kolbe began working with her when she was in a very critical state. She behaved extremely antisocially — pinching, biting, scratching — partly on purpose, partly she seemed to handle other people just like things. 'During this crisis it was impossible to develop a vocabulary with her. We just sat next to each other, I repeated her word fragments and reflected her behaviours. She was not aggressive at all. The atmosphere was peaceful and pleasant. I saw her two or three times a week. After six weeks, the symptoms had considerably diminished. It certainly helped that I did not expect anything from her and the sessions were just spent with contact.'

The psychologists are working on two levels. On the one hand individual therapies purposefully foster a person and offer her an opportunity to grow. On the other hand they also offer the staff a model. The therapy shows how things become possible for the disabled person which before she was not believed capable of. This is encouraging the staff sometimes to leave the established routine and respond to the residents differently. 'Sometimes tiny little things can move something,' is the experience of the two psychologists. It gives them satisfaction to observe the staff becoming gradually more open for the psychologists' concerns. Both agree that it would be important to offer the staff more training in this direction: 'Then, in many cases no individual therapy would be needed, but facilitating of growth could happen within the setting of the group's daily life.'

The chapter 'A hopeless case?' (Pörtner, 2000, pp. 105–13) describes an experience of another psychologist at Stetten, *Barbara Krietemeyer.* Based on her client-centred attitude — though at that time not yet knowing about Pre-Therapy — she has sensitively perceived and respected the very subtle directions of a severely disabled woman and patiently let herself be guided by those. This way she intuitively developed a way of working that was very close to the principles of Pre-Therapy. She succeeded in gradually breaking through the isolation of this woman, who had been completely encapsulated in herself, in gently establishing a relationship with her and in fostering her growth in a way that was just amazing. Nobody before would have believed that anything like that could be possible at all. It allowed the staff to discover other sides of this problematic person and to respond to her differently. Things became possible now that before were considered to be out of question.

4. In everyday care

I learned during my long-term activities as a staff consultant in different social organisations how important it is to encourage people with special needs in daily life and how suitable the person-centred approach is for doing so. Based on these experiences, in my book *Trust and Understanding* (Pörtner 1996a, 2000), I have developed a concept for person-centred work in social organisations and communities. From person-centred principles, guidelines are deduced for how to work in daily life with people who in some way or other need care or support, especially but not exclusively, people with mental disabilities. This concept includes elements of Pre-Therapy because nowhere are there so many opportunities to facilitate contact as in daily life. For confused elderly people, for example, establishing contact is of great help for getting better orientation in time and space. Contact reflections can easily be integrated into daily routine — such as having people washed, dressed, take a shower, set the table etc. — thus helping them to be more aware of what is happening with and around them. Besides reinforcing their contact functions it also helps to reduce anxiety when people are realising more clearly what is going on.

The concepts of trust and understanding are suited to improving life quality not only for the clients, but also for the carers working with them. To step out of dull routine, to discover and make use of our own personal resources for finding new and better ways of responding to the people we care for, is likely to make our caring more satisfying and less stressful.

Chapter 3

Concluding Thoughts

Pre-Therapy in the context of the Person-Centred Approach

Pre-Therapy cannot be separated from the Person-Centred Approach. It is built upon its fundamentals and has considerably contributed to its evolution.

This opinion is shared by the people with whom, in preparation for this book, I talked about their pre-therapeutic work. For Ton Coffeng Pre-Therapy represents 'a clear consequence of Carl Rogers. Garry made it more concrete and more explicit.' In addition he sees Pre-Therapy as 'a deepening of Gendlin's Experiencing and Focusing. It is a new process theory along the same lines as Gendlin's 'wisdom of the body'. Bart Santen, who says he learned a lot from Gestalt therapy too and does not consider himself a dogmatic client-centred therapist, agrees: 'Yes, I think Pre-Therapy belongs totally to that background . . . I cannot quite follow Garry when he refers to Perls and others and cannot see how he integrates that. Nor do I think these explanations are necessary. Pre-Therapy is valuable in itself.' It should be made clear that the parallels with Gestalt therapy and other approaches Prouty is pointing to in the first part of this book are always referring to *ways of thinking* and *theoretical concepts*. *The therapeutic practice of Pre-Therapy is clearly Client-Centred*, in fact Prouty even stays with the notion of 'non-directivity' (see p. 15 and Pörtner 1994, p. 38).

Dion Van Werde's description of the 'functioning in the grey zone' (see p. 81) shows clearly how much Pre-Therapy is a component of Client-Centred Psychotherapy. He points to the importance for a therapist of being able to sensitively recognise the client's level of functioning and to switch accordingly from contact reflections to 'regular' Client-Centred Therapy and vice versa. Also for integrating contact reflections into everyday situations and activities, a person-centred attitude is indispensable for recognising the level at which the other person is functioning and which kind of responses are appropriate at the moment.

Pre-Therapy is not only a component of the client-centred concept but in return, by making some of its implicit aspects more explicit and concrete, it has effects on it too. The concepts developed in Pre-Therapy — such as Van Werde's 'anchoring' — are helpful as well for considerations about psycho-therapy in general, about supervision or about the psychological balance of therapists and carers themselves. That Pre-Therapy, by reaching a group of persons who for a long time had been believed inaccessible for Client-Centred — or even any — Psychotherapy, represents an *enlargement* of the Client-Centred Approach is quite obvious. More of a surprise to me was to discover how Pre-Therapy can also be an *access* to the Person-Centred Approach. A number of people working in the social field, to whom up to then the Person-Centred Approach had not appealed, came to understand and appreciate it, through Pre-Therapy.

Moreover, in preparing this book, I met several professionals of different educational backgrounds who through Pre-Therapy for the first time came in touch with client-centred concepts. Having met Prouty and his work, some people, such as the movement therapist and other staff members at Sint-Amandus, though not explicitly working with Pre-Therapy, consequently tried to realise a person-centred attitude in their specific professional field.

Ton Coffeng observed the same in the context of his training activities. 'Through Prouty many people find access to and begin to understand the Client-Centred Approach.' Elke Lambers, who teaches counselling courses at Strathclyde University, Glasgow, where she also introduces Pre-Therapy to the participants, confirms this experience: 'Many students, through Pre-Therapy, immediately get access to a person-centred attitude. They are in the middle of their period of practical training and here they get something that they can concretely make use of.' And Hans Peters says, 'Through Pre-Therapy, for me the approach became concrete.'

'Concreteness' is an essential element that Pre-Therapy has contributed to the Client-Centred Approach or at least made explicit as one of its central aspects. Wim Lucieer points to the importance of being concrete: 'To be concrete is so important in psychotherapy. We have a tendency to become abstract. And then we lose the other person. It is important to stay absolutely concrete.' The Pre-Therapy team at Sint-Amandus too emphasises the importance of remaining 'concrete' while reflecting. 'To avoid interpretation is an extreme form of respect towards the experience of the client, a source of security within the contact' (Van Wyngene, Dumon and Coninckx, 2000).

Pre-Therapy is a concretisation and an enlargement of the Client-Centred/ Person-Centred Approach. With the contact reflections it offers concrete handles of action. Yet Pre-Therapy goes beyond reflections.

Reflections
Reflections are an indispensable method element of Pre-Therapy because 'the use of reflections helps to develop a person-centred attitude,' as Hans Peters has put it earlier. Yet they should never be used in a mechanical way, and they alone do not make Pre-Therapy. 'The concept of Pre-Therapy is broader than just the reflections. Yet they help and train to listen,' is Wim Lucieer's opinion.

Contact reflections are an instrument to facilitate contact and at the same time help the therapist or carer to develop a person-centred attitude. Just as in Client-Centred Psychotherapy 'repeating what I have understood' is not a mechanical 'mirroring' (this too is a frequent misunderstanding), but an instrument to 'feel into' the world of the other person, which at the same time is fostering the development and consolidation of a therapeutic attitude. Therefore reflections are firmly established in Client-Centred Psychotherapy. But just as in Pre-Therapy, the essential is the person-centred attitude. However, there is another important aspect to reflections that should not be underestimated: they are a particularly helpful instrument, also in daily life, to facilitate the clients' contact with their experiencing.

Reflections have to be used in subtle ways. Never should they make the other person feel belittled or silly. People with special needs are reacting very touchy when their ticks are reflected. Persons with mild disabilities in particular might feel it strange when their words or body movements are reflected. Communication has to be always on the same level of contact where the client is at the moment. Contact reflections are appropriate when the client's contact (to reality, to herself, to others) is interrupted or not there. As soon as contact is established, the level of communication will change. There are flowing transitions to client-centred responses in psychotherapy, or to conversation in daily life.

It frequently happens that people, after having participated in one or two seminars with Prouty, still feel insecure about how to use contact reflections concretely. If the first attempts are not quite successful, they loose courage and let it go. There is a need for follow up training programmes that emphasise the methodical differentiation and the transfer into the specific working situations of each participant.

Outlook

There is a remarkable variety of ways to use Pre-Therapy. For some professionals it is predominantly a way to deal with acute crisis situations; for others it is not only that, but also an essential component of the therapeutic process. Others again use it to establish contact in daily life. All these different applications show the wide range of possibilities for Pre-Therapy and suggest that its potential is still far from being exhausted. We hope that the described examples will motivate people who already work with Pre-Therapy to exchange their experiences and to further develop their own ways of application. The different ways to integrate Pre-Therapy in different activities that Dion Van Werde describes, might stimulate creative ideas for the reader's own field of activity.

Impressive changes can be observed with chronic psychiatric patients who practically had been 'given up'. That it is possible to break through the isolation they have been caught in for years or even decades, that human beings who for twenty years did not speak, and then start to tell others things about themselves, is amazing. Even if for most of these long-term patients it is too late to fundamentally change their life situation, small steps (often by outsiders wrongly considered as unimportant) might contribute to significantly improving the quality of their lives — which in return will make work more satisfying for the carers. Moreover such experiences are of value because they prove that much more could be achieved and negative effects of hospitalisation significantly reduced, if patients from the beginning are responded to in this way. As the Pre-Therapy team in Beernem remarked: 'Perhaps then it would happen less frequently, that in addition to the initial disease, twice as severe disorders are developing at the hospital.'

This does not necessarily ask for additional financial means, but, above all, for a shift in thinking. However, this appears to be difficult for many people, not only among the staff, but also for the management and the authorities who take the decisions. They often have not enough contact with patients or residents to get a clear idea of their problems and — under pressure of necessary financial restrictions — sometimes make decisions that appear reasonable written on paper, but do not take into account the reality of daily life in the organisations concerned.

For the staff, to step out of a routine that is perhaps a little dull but also in some ways easy, is not just a stimulating challenge. Such a shift in thinking also raises fears. Many things have to be questioned that up to then had appeared solid and certain. Their own capabilities, convictions and motivations have to be considered anew. This is not always easy and even becomes threatening when all of a sudden doubts arise about their competence. The staff therefore must be offered the necessary support and further training. In this regard some investments are necessary that will surely have great benefits in the future.

It is crucial to consider the *frame of reference of the staff,* to take seriously their fears and reservations and to meet them where they are. This often is not sufficiently taken into consideration by those who themselves are convinced of this new way of working and want to convince others. Their eagerness to improve the situation for the clients is quite understandable, but sometimes results in a lack of empathy towards reluctant staff members. However, only if those too are understood in their difficult situation, will new perspectives open up.

A similar attitude is needed towards the organisation with its established structures, in order to make change possible. 'We have to be empathic also with the system, then a lot is possible,' is Dion Van Werde's experience (Pörtner 2000, p. 91). And his achievements prove that he is right. We see it happen again and again that organisations immediately resist innovations if we do not pay attention to their reality. Just as with an individual, we first of all have to understand the situation as it is, and from there try to develop options for change. We also have to acknowledge those conditions that must be taken for granted. In terms of the general setting of an organisation too, we have to consider the 'balance between structure and freedom' (Pörtner 1996, 2000).

However, it is not always easy to be empathic with a system that we perceive as inadequate, particularly if there is a lot of pressure, for example because of austerity measures. Such measures that sometimes considerably impair the residents' well-being and impede the staff's work, often rebound and end up costing more, instead of less.

This is equally true with time. In most organisations the staff are under constant pressure of time, and therefore afraid of anything that could add to it. Yet, the changes we suggest do not ask for more time, but for setting other priorities. Listening carefully and responding to a person for a minute is often more effective than trying to influence her for fifteen minutes. To take a moment to become aware of how a person feels might make unnecessary many a stressful dispute that consumes time and energy. Moreover, as we have seen, very often this way can prevent a person's condition getting worse. This also saves time, even if initially some time has to be invested. Unfortunately professionals frequently do not recognise how this is connected and consider working in person-centred and pre-therapeutic ways to be a waste of time. 'Though in the long term it would be much more efficient and even time saving,' is Wim Lucieer convinced. Dion Van Werde's work proves clearly how, without asking for more time or more staff, the person-centred attitude and pre-therapeutic concepts can be integrated into the regular daily routine of a psychiatric ward.

What we need is a broad, holistic, long-term view that does not observe each task and the time it takes isolated from the context. A concept emphasising the well-being and individuality of the persons cared for, and at the same time allowing the staff to experience their work as useful and satisfying, a concept fostering and making use of the resources of all the people involved, in the long term will probably even save time and money. Yet, this should not be the only criterion regarding care for ill, old or disabled persons. It is the respect for the dignity of each human being that we have to ensure by the way we are working.

Part 3 References and Bibliography

Binder, U. (1994a) *Empathieentwicklung und Pathogenese in der klientenzentrierten Psychotherapie.* Eschborn: Klotz.

Binder, U. (1994b) Klientenzentrierte Psychotherapie mit Patienten aus dem schizophrenen Formenkreis. In Hutterer-Krisch, R. (ed.) *Psychotherapie mit psychotischen Menschen.* Vienna: Springer Verlag.

Binder, U. (1996) Die Bedeutung des motivationalen Aspektes von Empathie und kognitiver sozialer Perspektivenübernahme in der personzentrierten Psychotherapie. In Hutterer, R., Pawlowsky, G., Schmid, P.F., Stipsits,R. (eds.) *Client-Centered and Experiential Psychotherapy: A paradigm in motion.* Frankfurt a. M.: Peter Lang, pp. 347–62.

Binder, U. and Binder, J. (1994) *Studien zu einer störungsspezifischen klientenzentrierten Psychotherapie – Schizophrene Ordnung – Psychosomatisches Erleben – Depressives Leiden.* 2. Aufl. Eschborn: Klotz.

Coffeng, T. (1994) The delicate approach to early trauma. In Hutterer, R., Pawlowsky, G., Schmid, P.F., Stipsits, R. (eds.) *Client-Centered and Experiential Psychotherapy: A paradigm in motion.* pp 499–511. Frankfurt a. M.: Peter Lang.

Coffeng, T. (1995) Pre-experiential approach to early trauma. In Esser, U., Pabst, H., Speierer, G-W. (eds.) *The Power of the Client-Centered Approach.* Cologne: GwG Verlag, pp. 185–203.

Coffeng, T. (1996) Pre-experiential contact to trauma. Lecture and video tape. Vienna: 1st International Conference of the World Council of Psychotherapy.

Coffeng, T. (1997) Pre-experiential contact with dissociation. Lecture and video tape. Lisbon: IVth International Conference for Client-Centered and Experiential Psychotherapy.

Coninckx, B., Dumon, L. and Van Wyngene, C. (1995) Persongerichte Conctact benadering. Jaarverslag van het Psychiatrisch Centrum Sint-Amandus, Beernem.

Leyssen, M. and Roelens, L. (1988) Herstel van contact-functies bij zwaar gestoorde patiënten door middel van Prouty's pre-therapie. In *Tijdschrift Klinische Psychologie, 18* (1), 21–34.

Peters, H. (1984) *Client-centered therapie en gedragstherapie: een aanzet tot integratie.* Lisse: Swets and Zeitlinger.

Peters, H. (1986a) Prouty's pretherapie methode en de behandeling van hallucinaties: een verslag. *Ruit, Multidisciplinair Tijdschrift voor Ontwikkelingsstoornissen, Zwakzinnigheid en Zwakzinnigenzorg, 12,* (1), 26-35. *Medelingenblad Vereniging voor Rogeriaanse Therapie, 2,* 34-46.

Peters, H. (1986b) Client-centered benaderingswijzen in de zwakzinnigenzorg. In: van Balen, R., Leijssen, M. and Lietaer, G. (eds.) *Droom en Werkelijkheid in Client-centered Psychotherapie.* Leuven/Amersfoort: Acco.

Peters, H. (1992a)*Psychotherapie bij geestelijk gehandicapten.* Lisse: Swets and Zeitlinger. German edition (2001) *Psychotherapeutische Zugänge zu Menschen mit geistiger Behinderung.* Stuttgart: Klett-Cotta.

Peters, H. (1992b) Personzentriertes Handeln in der Therapie geistig Behinderter. *GwG Zeitschrift 86,* 16-21.

Peters, H. (1996) Toepassing van Prouty's pretherapeutische methodes in de behandeling van geestelijk gehandicapten. In:*Tijdschrift voor Orthopedagogiek, Kinderpsychiatrie en Klinische Kinderpsychologie, 21,* 1, 2-13.

Peters, H. (1999a) Pre-therapy: a client-centered/experiential approach to mentally handicapped people. *Journal of Humanistic Psychology, 39,* (4).

Peters, H. (1999b) Client-centred therapy in the care of the mentally handicapped. *The Person-centered Journal, 6,* 164–78.

Pfeiffer, W. (1993) Die Bedeutung der Beziehung bei der Enstehung und Therapie von psychotischen Störungen. In Teusch, L. and Finke, J. (eds.) *Krankheitslehre in der Gesprächspsychotherapie.* Heidelberg, Asanger.

Pörtner, M. (1990) Client-Centered Psychotherapy with Mentally Retarded Persons: Catherine and Ruth. In Lietaer, G., Rombauts, J. and Van Balen, R. (eds.) *Client-Centered and Experiential Psychotherapy in the Nineties,* pp. 659-69. Leuven: Leuven University Press. German (1984) Gesprächstherapie mit geistig behinderten Klienten. *GwG-Info 56,* 20–30, *Brennpunkt 11,* 6–23.

Pörtner, M. (1994) *Praxis der Gesprächspsychotherapie, Interviews mit Therapeuten,* Stuttgart: Klett Cotta.

Pörtner, M. (1996) *Ernstnehmen – Zutrauen – Verstehen. Personzentrierte Haltung im Umgang mit geistig behinderten und pflegebedürftigen Menschen.* Stuttgart: Klett-Cotta. Dutch edition (1998) *Serieus nemen, vertrouwen, begrijpen,* Maarssen: Elsevier/De Tijdstrom. Danish edition (in press) Copenhagen: Hans Reitzels Publishers.

Pörtner, M. (1996a) Garry Prouty's Konzept der Prä-Therapie. *Wege zur seelischen Gesundheit für Menschen mit geistiger Behinderung: Psychotherapie und Persönlichkeitsentwicklung,* 216–26. Bern: Huber.

Pörtner, M. (1996b) Working with the Mentally Handicapped in a Person-Centered Way — is it possible, is it appropriate and what does it mean in practice? In Hutterer, R., Pawlowsky, G., Schmid, P.F. and Stipsits, R. (eds.) *Client-Centered and Experiential Psychotherapy, A paradigm in motion,* p. 513-27. Frankfurt a. M.: Peter Lang.

Pörtner, M. (2000) *Trust and Understanding: the Person-Centred Approach to everyday care for people with special needs.* Ross-on-Wye: PCCS Books.

Roelens, L. (1989) Samenvatting van de theoretische en technische basisbegrippen van Prouty's pre-therapie. Prouty's pre-therapy: theoretical and technical core concepts: a summary. Script, Beernem, Psychiatrisch Centrum Sint-Amandus.

Santen, B. (1988) Focusing with a borderline adolescent. *Person-Centred Review,* 3, 442–62.

Santen, B. (1990) Beyond good and evil: Focusing with early traumatized children and adolescents. In: Lietaer, G., Rombauts, J. and van Balen, R. (eds) *Client-Centered and Experiential Psychotherapy in the Nineties.* 779-96. Leuven: Leuven University Press. German (1990a) Jenseits von Gut und Böse. Erlebniswelt eines 12-jährigen und seine Veränderung — Ein Dokument. *GwG-Zeitschrift, 21,* (78), 55-9.

Santen, B. (1993) Focusing with a dissociated adolescent: tracing and treating multiple personality disorder experienced by a 13-year old girl. *Folio, a journal for focusing and experiential psychotherapy,* 12, (2), 45–58.

Santen, B. (1995) Focusing met een gedissocieerde adolescent; enn meervoudige identiteitsstoornis bij en 13-jarig meisje. In Lietaer, G. and van Kalmthout, M. (eds.) *Praktijkboek gesprekstherapie. Psychopathologie en expërientiële procesbevordering,* 267–76. Utrecht: De Tijdstroom.

Van Wyngene, C. (1996) *Cliëntgerichte benadering van chronisch schizofrenecliënten.* Turnhout, Specialisatieverslag Faculteit voor Mens en Samenleving.

Van Wyngene, C., Dumon, L. and Coninckx, B. (2000) Working to establish contact: how contact reflections can initiate a process. *Tijdschrift voor hulpverleners in de geestelijke gezondheidzorg, 17, (2),* 165–78.

The largest list of Client-Centred Therapy and Person-Centred Approach books in the world

Client Centred Therapy and the Person Centred Approach
Essential Readers
Series Edited by Tony Merry

Person-Centred Therapy: A revolutionary paradigm
Jerold Bozarth

Experiences in Relatedness: Groupwork and the person-centred approach
Colin Lago & Mhairi MacMillan (Eds)

Women Writing in the Person-Centred Approach
Irene Fairhurst (Ed)

Understanding Psychotherapy: Fifty years of client-centred theory and practice
C.H.Patterson

The Person-Centred Approach: A passionate presence
Peggy Natiello

Family, Self and Psychotherapy: A person-centred perspective
Ned L. Gaylin

Rogers' Therapeutic Conditions: Evolution, Theory and Practice
Series Edited by Gill Wyatt

Volume 1: Congruence — Gill Wyatt (Ed)

Volume 2: Empathy — Sheila Haugh & Tony Merry (Eds)

Volume 3: Unconditional Positive Regard — Jerold Bozarth & Paul Wilkins (Eds)

Volume 4: Contact and Perception — Gill Wyatt & Pete Sanders (Eds)

Voices of the Voiceless: Person-centred approaches to people
with learning disabilities
Jan Hawkins

Trust and Understanding: The person-centred approach to everyday care for
people with special needs
Marlis Pörtner

visit our website for news of the latest person-centred releases
www.pccs-books.co.uk
UK customers call 01989 77 07 07 for discounts